ARTISTS AND WRITERS

ARTISTS AND WRITERS

Nineteenth and Twentieth Century Portrait Drawings from the Collection of Benjamin Sonnenberg. Catalogue by Felice Stampfle and Cara Dufour. With an Introduction by Brendan Gill.

The Pierpont Morgan Library, New York

May 13 to July 30, 1971

29 EAST 36 STREET · NEW YORK, N.Y. 10016

Library of Congress Catalogue Card Number 73-161537

ISBN 87598-004-X

PRINTED IN THE UNITED STATES OF AMERICA

PREFACE

MR. BENJAMIN SONNENBERG, in his house on Gramercy Park or on the sidewalks of New York, is one of the well-known figures of this city. Saul Steinberg's drawing of him, which accompanied Geoffrey Hellman's profile of Mr. Sonnenberg in *The New Yorker* for April 8, 1950, and is included in this catalogue, catches the man precisely: bowler-hatted, mustachioed, an eternal Edwardian. He steps forth into the glare and jangle of the twentieth century, which he has helped to shape, but he remains as Mr. Hellman has written, "a robust, arresting anachronism."

Mr. Sonnenberg is a witty and a wise talker and the excitement of his collecting scintillates in his conversation, as does his collection itself in the town house on the park. Mr. Steinberg has shown only the essences of this collection in his drawing – only the spirit of the superlative furniture, the hundreds of pieces of brass, the paintings, sculptures, china, glass and silver. Man and house and collection are really one. Mr. Mahonri Sharp Young has accurately written that "in many ways the most remarkable thing in the collection is the collector himself, who has made so many other men famous."

It is therefore very difficult to take any part of Mr. Sonnenberg's world away from the house on Gramercy Park without doing the collector and the collection an injustice. The portrait drawings form only one of the many groups of drawings in his collection, which ranges from the early sixteenth century to the present. The rich surrounding gives every drawing in the house a special authority in its own place, and may make it seem somehow diminished when removed from the house. Yet when the environment is so "swagger" – to use one of Mr. Sonnenberg's favorite words – many of these intimate studies may also be passed over. By collecting them together in one place we have a clearer view of the artistic world of the last one hundred fifty years and we can assess the achievement of those years in informal portraiture as we cannot in the house itself. It is therefore hoped that by concentrating on one aspect of Mr. Sonnenberg's collection these portrait drawings of artists and writers, their families and friends, will reinforce each other and bring to life a rather neglected aspect of nineteenth- and twentieth-century art.

In his reading and conversation Mr. Sonnenberg has always indicated a preference for biography and essays. These portrait drawings were chosen by a man who loves Hazlitt. They are really biographical sketches. They are not literary art, in the sense of being illustrative, descriptive, or anecdotal; they are not pictorial translation of verbal ideas. Mr. Sonnenberg in his collecting has avoided almost all the literary pictorialism in English art (or in French art), whether it be that of Hogarth's London, the apocalypse or pastoral dream of Blake's or Palmer's Shoreham, or the Pre-Raphaelite allegory. He has not collected narrative pictures, and the portraits in his collection do not call up historical or legendary antecedents. They are incisive studies of creative men and women of purpose and intelligence. Many of the women shown here, if not ugly, are at least homely; but they have a quickness which is none the less alluring. They are vital, if not beautiful. There are few temptresses, but any number who would make excellent company at a dinner table.

The ties between literature and art go back and forth: artists drawing writers or other artists or themselves. The French representation is strong: drawings by most of the artists of importance between 1800 and 1930 are illustrated. Picasso is, perhaps, the most notable omission. The English Regency is there, but no works from the Romantic worlds which include Fuseli and Blake. Very few of the drawings come from countries outside of France, England, and America. The heart of the collection, as one might expect from what has been said of the collector himself, is the Edwardian world and its immediate afterglow. "The Silver Age" of English art, 1890-1928, is shown in every aspect of its literary and artistic interests. From there it is one easy step to a similar American world of critical cultivation: George Santayana and Edmund Wilson.

These portrait drawings, with a few exceptions, are of people who are as interesting as the artists who drew them. The notes in the catalogue therefore often focus on the sitter. The subjects of two of the finest drawings may not be recognized, however, and may not even be accepted as portrait drawings: those by Van Gogh and Seurat. But these two drawings reveal such total mastery of technique and understanding of character that from the backs of the subjects alone the artists have created what are surely profoundly moving portraits.

Mr. Sonnenberg's collection of portrait drawings begins with the striking profile drawing of a man (about 1500), now generally attributed to Bernadino dei Conti. The strength of the Sonnenberg collection, however, is clearly in the period covered by this catalogue.

The drawings were selected and the catalogue was prepared by Miss Felice Stampfle, Curator of Drawings and Prints, and Miss Cara Dufour, assisted by Mrs. Ruth Kraemer. They were helped in every way by Mr. Sonnenberg himself and by his secretary, Miss Jeanette Blader. The introduction to the catalogue was written by Mr. Brendan Gill, a close friend of Mr. Sonnenberg and formerly Chairman of the Council of Fellows of The Pierpont Morgan Library. It seems to me appropriate that these portraits of artists and writers should first be shown as a group in this Library, which has a great archive of literary autographs and the finest collection of old master drawings in America. Mr. Sonnenberg's collection, as shown, more or less begins where that of the Morgan Library leaves off. It is therefore especially welcome in this Library, where for a number of years Mr. Sonnenberg has been a good friend, and where he is at present a member of the Council of Fellows.

CHARLES RYSKAMP, *Director*

NUMBER NINETEEN
GRAMERCY PARK

"FIRST OF ALL" is a phrase much favored by the Master of Number Nineteen. Mr. Sonnenberg has an exceptionally quick mind, which he slows down for the convenience of others by turning ordinary discourse into a game of cat and mouse, with himself playing both roles. In such a game, a phrase like "first of all" serves to entice a listener and yet keep him at bay. Mr. Sonnenberg will often use it to introduce one or another of his scores of entertaining cautionary tales, self-interrupted from time to time by asides that bristle with names, dates, and voluptuously veiled hints of the never-to-be-wholly-explained. These labyrinthine asides, emphasized by prolonged silences, fixed stares under quizzically lifted brows, and a dozen procrastinative ritual gestures of pipe-cleaning, pipe-filling, pipe-lighting, and pipe-smoking, themselves gradually acquire asides; in the mind of the hypnotized listener, they give the impression that they are accumulating strings of footnote-like dependencies, making the smoky blue air about Mr. Sonnenberg's head seem to sparkle with asterisks, daggers, brackets, virgules and ☞ ☞ ☞.

First of all, then, as Mr. Sonnenberg would say, we will speak of the Park, and there are reasons. For one thing, it is, like so many of Mr. Sonnenberg's own so-called "bits," a rarity: the only private park in the city. For another, it isn't truly a park but a square — a demure and shapely private square, whose bounds can be nimbly paced off in a matter of minutes and whose modest adornments, observable through locked gates, grant an almost equal pride of place to a small bronze statue of Edwin Booth and a large green-and-white gabled wooden birdhouse on a pole. A third reason to speak of the Park is that it puts off for a moment the opportunity to speak of Mr. Sonnenberg, who, though he rejoices to pay compliments, is made miserable by having to receive them. His feelings in this regard deserve attention; praise delayed will please him not because it is praise but because it is delayed. The eccentric elegance of his dress and the extravagance of his hospitality have made him one of the most readily recognizable men in New York and on the Continent, but it appears that he has chosen to be conspicuous in the hope of rendering himself invisible. Like many of the artists and writers whose works he cherishes, he would prefer to be at once famous and unknown.

So we begin with the Park, glancing sidelong at it before we approach the big black door of Number Nineteen, with its polished brass lion-headed knocker glowering not in the least fiercely at us in the paneled vestibule. (According to Mr. Sonnenberg, when he took title to the house and discovered that the vestibule, having been built in part on what was properly sidewalk, belonged in part to the city and not to him, he came close to bursting into tears. To have worked as hard as he had in order to possess a kingdom, and then not to possess *all* of it!) Gramercy Park looks back over its shoulder to England, and so does Number Nineteen, and so does its Master. They are, those three, so they strike us as saying, precisely where they wish to be, and it is only by some curious geographical and chronological mishap that the place should happen to be New York and not London and the time the twentieth century instead of the nineteenth. Mr. and Mrs. Sonnenberg have been at Number Nineteen for forty years, Number Nineteen has been on the Park for just over a hundred years, and the Park itself has existed for almost a hundred and fifty years; these count as long periods in a city notorious for its habit of incessantly building itself up and tearing itself down. Decade after decade, the Park has spread a leafy benignity at the foot of Lexington Avenue, in the heart of the city and yet isolated from the grim gridiron of speculator-built blocks flowing past it in endless self-imitation up the island. A few tall buildings reached the borders of the Park in the nineteen twenties and thirties, but a remarkable number of splendid old houses survive, casting over the neighborhood what Henry James would call the incomparable tone of time. Of these houses, some have been turned into apartments and others into clubs – Edwin Booth's house, at Number Sixteen, has long been the Players Club and the Tilden house next door is the headquarters of the National Arts Club – while a few remain, simply and grandly, private residences.

Number Nineteen, on the Southeast corner of Twentieth Street and Irving Place, is not only the greatest private house on the Park: at the moment of writing, it is surely the greatest private house left in New York. Local history books often identify it as the Mrs. Stuyvesant Fish mansion, in tribute to the original owner. Like the Sonnenbergs, Mrs. Fish loved giving parties; for a century now, passersby have seen the windows of the great house ablaze with candles far, far into the night. If one includes a wing of the house running South along Irving Place, which the Sonnenbergs added some years ago in place of the Fish carriage house, Number Nineteen contains upwards of forty rooms – enough, one would think, for all practical purposes, especially since the two Sonnenberg children are grown and have establishments elsewhere in the city. The face of the building is in the style of the Second Empire, with walls of rosy red brick, black trim at the windows, and a steep dormered mansard roof, displaying at its highest point a merriment of painted iron fretwork against the sky. The house does not so much dominate the Park as with amiable augustness preside over it, sharing what amounts to the pleasant task of host with such neighbors as the lanterned and balconied Players to the West and the conscientiously uningratiating Friends Meeting House to the East. (It deserves to be mentioned in passing that the Meeting House owes its continued presence on the Park to the alertness and generosity of Mr. Sonnenberg and two or three suggestible friends, who, on learning that the property had been sold and that a high-rise apartment house was to go up in its place, purchased the building and secured its preservation as a historic landmark.)

Despite the awesome abundance of rooms in Number Nineteen, one's first impression on stepping past the lion-headed knocker into the broad, low-ceilinged, oyster-white front hall is that of a cozy homeliness: of one's having been quite unexpectedly ushered into some delightful snug cave of a country house, ample and opulent and yet taking care to be more comfortable than opulent. Deliciously and mysteriously – a mystery that never diminishes with familiarity – the air smells of spices, and the old parquet gives up out of its waxed, dusky depths reflections of innumerable brass objects of every size and purpose: buckets, caskets, candlesticks, and graduated pound weights are what come to mind afterward, when one tries to recapture the initial bedazzlement. To the left of the front door is a small, dark-paneled room, whose deeply embrasured windows look out at ground level onto the Park, and in whose handsome fireplace (an improvement of the early eighteen nineties?) one wonders, even in mid-summer, whether a fire hasn't just gone out, for standing by it one catches the bittersweet scent of woodsmoke, mingled with that of the flowers that are everywhere in the house. Many friends of the Sonnenbergs call this little room, filled with books and drawings and with, here and there, something silvery winking in the shadows, their favorite; it is as satisfactory of its kind as the large red and white confectionary ballroom on the fifth floor, which also looks out over the Park but from a height and therefore with a difference.

In the good old-fashioned way, Number Nineteen gains in grandeur as it rises, but the house is a chapter in an unwritten book, or is perhaps itself a book, in which every room becomes a chapter, and we must be resolute in not setting foot on even so much as the first tread of the great staircase that mounts, landing by landing, with a balustrade as sturdy and welcoming to the hand as the deck-rail of some eighteenth-century galleon, through the trophy-filled heart of the house. The intention here has been to give the viewer of the pictures in this exhibition a glimpse of the happy setting from which, for a happy reason, they have been borrowed, and to give a glimpse, too, of the man who has collected them – a humorous, graceful, bookish, learned man, who, for all his confidence in the many disguises he wears (he pretends to be gregarious and is a contented solitary), is not above letting us see that he is aware of the implications of his lifelong passion for collecting. Number Nineteen is the prize that Mr. Sonnenberg has wrested from the world, but it would be but the crudest "first of all" of a cautionary tale unworthy of his high standard for us to turn this extraordinary achievement into a conventional American success story. It is indeed wonderful that Mr. Sonnenberg could have arrived in this country as a boy of thirteen, speaking no English and totally without means, and be settled in Number Nineteen by the age of thirty, but the victory that this implies is more complicated than it looks. Number Nineteen is not a monument to Mr. Sonnenberg's success in a profession – public relations – that he helped to invent but has never, one guesses, learned to admire; having described himself as a builder of plinths for other men to stand on, Mr. Sonnenberg has reason to preserve a certain scepticism towards monuments. The simplest truth is that Number Nineteen is a work of art that holds and enfolds many works of art, and it holds and enfolds Mr. Sonnenberg as well. It is the beautiful house he lives in, among beautiful things; what it may be to him more than that is for him to reveal. As Henri Focillon wrote long ago, telling of how art had filled his days, "I have lived in it as a familiar and strange world, not for mere luxury or the easy satisfactions of sensibility, not to classify it like a collection of shells, but first of all to be happy in it, to find there through noble things that interior growth which we need – to find a life both actual and supernatural, whose most brilliant manifestations keep the privilege of secrecy."

BRENDAN GILL

CATALOGUE
OF THE EXHIBITION

Catalogue of the Exhibition

JACQUES-LOUIS DAVID

PARIS 1748 - BRUSSELS 1825

1 POPE PIUS VII (Gregorio Luigi Barnaba Chiaramonti) 1742 - 1823

Pencil. 8⅛ x 7¼ inches.
Lettered in pencil at lower center: *PIE VII*; below, somewhat illegibly inscribed in pencil: *Pie Sept.*
Verso: Study of two heads.

The features of Pius VII are well-known from the paintings of Ingres (1814) and Sir Thomas Lawrence (1819) but perhaps most familiar in David's portrait of the pontiff painted in 1805 when the latter was in his sixty-third year. The pope made his historic visit to Paris in 1804 to consecrate Napoleon's coronation on December 2 in the cathedral of Notre-Dame. In the end, however, it was Napoleon who placed the crown upon his own head. The emperor, anxious to point up the *rapprochement* between his new imperial regime and the Vatican, induced the pope to remain in the French capital for four months. Towards the end of his visit, while lodged in the Tuileries, Pius sat to the emperor's painter David, and this drawing probably is one of the artist's preliminary studies for the great portrait now in the Louvre.

The painter remarked of the pope:

> "Ce bon vieillard, quelle figure vénérable! . . . Comme il est simple . . . et quelle belle tête il a! Une tête bien italienne, l'enchassement de l'oeil grand, bien prononcé! Celui-là est vraiment un pape. . . . Il est pauvre comme Saint Pierre; les dorures de ses habits sont fausses! . . ."

Provenance: Mme Mongez (according to Destailleur sale); Hippolyte Destailleur (sale, Paris, "Vente Hippolyte Destailleur," May 26–27, 1893, p. 7, no. 30).

Exhibitions: Toulouse, Musée des Augustins, "Ingres et ses Maîtres de Roques à David," 1955, p. 61, no. 62; Charleroi, Palais des Beaux-Arts, "Exposition Fragonard, David, Navez," 1957, p. 43, no. 33.

PIERRE-PAUL PRUD'HON

CLUNY 1758 - PARIS 1823

2 COUNT SOMMARIVA. d. 1828

Black and white chalk, stumped, on blue-gray paper. 9⅝ x 6¾ inches.

Signed (signature concealed by mount) in black chalk at lower left: *P. P. Prud'hon.*

As Delacroix remarked of Prud'hon, "Charm and grace will always be the hallmark of his talent," and the lyric mood is evident in the woodland setting of the painted portrait of Giovanni Battista Sommariva completed in 1815 and now in the Brera Gallery, Milan. The count, who came of an old Lombard family, had sided with the French when they invaded Italy in 1796, and he served on the directorate of the Cisalpine Republic until 1802, at which time he moved to Paris. There he made his fortune through speculation and settled down to a life of art patronage. His collection, which was famous at the time, included important Prud'hon works. The painted portrait, exhibited in its unfinished state in the salon of 1814, was preceded by a number of preparatory drawings. The Sonnenberg sheet comes late in the sequence.

Provenance: Camille Marcille (sale, Paris, Hôtel Drouot, 1876, no. 130); Camille Groult (sale, Paris, Galerie Charpentier, no. 49, pl. XXII).

Bibliography: Edmond de Goncourt, *Catalogue raisonné de l'oeuvre de P. P. Prud'hon*, Paris, 1876, pp. 43, 323; Jean Guiffrey, "L'Oeuvre de Pierre-Paul Prud'hon," *Archives de l'Art Français*, Nouvelle Periode, XIII, 1924, p. 235, no. 620; Agnes Mongan in *Great Drawings of All Times*, III, 1962, no. 713, repr.; Mahonri Sharp Young, "Treasures in Gramercy Park," *Apollo*, LXXXV, 1967, p. 181.

Exhibitions: Chartres, Société Archéologique d'Eure-et-Loire, "Exposition Archéologique et d'Objects d'Art," 1858, no. 91; Paris, Ecole des Beaux-Arts, 1874, no. 140; Paris, "Exposition Universelle de 1900," Retrospective de la Ville de Paris.

SIR THOMAS LAWRENCE

BRISTOL 1769 - LONDON 1830

3 GEORGE IV. 1762 - 1830

Black chalk, heightened with white and red chalk, on buff-tinted canvas.
16½ x 14½ inches.

George IV ruled England as regent from 1811 until his father's death in 1820 when he acceded to the throne. During the Regency and afterwards, the "first gentleman of Europe," as he was called, continued as the "leader in all license and luxury." Although he was not popular as a monarch, contemporary diarists speak of his considerable charm and taste. A great collector of French works of art, he also interested himself in the architecture and decoration of Carleton House and the Pavilion at Brighton. He himself executed architectural and decorative designs.

The king sat to Lawrence for six different portraits, of which Kenneth Garlick has counted at least thirty-three replicas and copies indicating something of the demand for the king's likeness. "I saw a room full of them," remarked the sixth Duke of Devonshire on a visit to Kensington Palace in 1845. On the other hand, drawings of the subject are quite rare. The example shown here is apparently a study for the full-length portrait of the future king executed in 1815 for Lord Charles Stewart, now in the collection of the Marquess of Londonderry.

Provenance: François Flameng (L. 1030); Flameng sale, Paris, Galerie Georges Petit, 1919, no. 135; Vicomte de Canson; Mayer Collection, Paris; Mrs. Coggeshall Kuhn, Washington, D.C. (on loan to Fogg Art Museum, 1961).

Bibliography: Kenneth Garlick, "A catalogue of the paintings, drawings and pastels of Sir Thomas Lawrence," *The Walpole Society*, XXXIX, 1962 – 1964, p. 227 f., no. 2.

JEAN-AUGUSTE-DOMINIQUE INGRES

MONTAUBAN 1780 - PARIS 1867

4 MONSIEUR AND MADAME EDME RAMEL

Pencil, heightened with white chalk, on wove paper. 13½ x 10⅝ inches.

Inscribed by the artist at lower center: *à mon cher frere Edmond Ramel / Souvenir de Cannes. J. Ingres / 1855*. Inscribed at the upper right: *Portraits de M^r et M^e Ed. Ramel.*

Edme-Marie-Dominique Ramel (ca. 1817 – 1875), shown here with his wife, Jeanne-Faustine-Marie-Irma-Donbernard (ca. 1821 – 1898), was the brother of Ingres' third wife, Delphine Ramel, whom he married in 1852 when he was seventy-one. The double portrait was drawn three years later when Ingres and his wife visited the Ramels at Cannes. M. Ramel was a customs collector in Cannes so it is appropriate that he should be seen against a coastal view with the mountains of L'Esterel in the distance. In the same year, perhaps on the same occasion, Ingres also drew portraits of his wife and her sister Mathilde.

Provenance: Edme Ramel; Madame Edme Ramel; Henri Haro (sale, Paris, February 3, 1912, no. 41, repr.); Henry Lapauze (sale, Paris, Hôtel Drouot, June 21, 1929, no. 34, repr.).

Bibliography: Henry Lapauze, *Les Portraits dessinés de J. A. D. Ingres*, Paris, 1903, p. 68, no. 78; Henry Lapauze, *Ingres, sa vie et son oeuvre*, Paris, 1911, p. 476; Henry Lapauze, *Jean Briant paysagiste, maître de Ingres, et le paysage dans l'oeuvre de Ingres*, Paris, 1911, p. 48; *Kunst und Künstler*, XXVII, July, 1929, repr. p. 408; Mahonri Sharp Young, "Treasures in Gramercy Park," *Apollo*, LXXXV, 1967, p. 178, fig. 10.

Exhibitions: Paris, Galerie Georges Petit, "Ingres," 1911, no. 173; London, Rosenberg and Helft, "Ten French Painters of the XIX Century," 1938, no. 11; New York, Paul Rosenberg, "Ingres in American Collections," 1961, no. 55; Poughkeepsie, New York, Vassar College, "Drawings and Watercolors from Alumnae and Their Families," 1961, no. 69, repr.; Cambridge, Mass., Fogg Art Museum, "Ingres Centennial Exhibition 1867-1967," 1967, no. 105, repr.; New York Metropolitan Museum of Art, Prints and Drawings Galleries, "Classicism and Romanticism, French Drawings and Prints 1800-1860," 1970, no. 58.

EUGENE DELACROIX

CHARENTON-ST. MAURICE 1798 - PARIS 1863

5 SEATED YOUNG WOMAN

Watercolor and gouache over pencil, some black and blue chalk. 11¼ x 9 inches.
Stamped in red at lower right: *E. D.* (Lugt 838).

The subject of this portrait has been associated with the girl whom Delacroix alternately referred to in his journal between 1822 and 1824 as "J" or "La Cara," a married woman with whom it would appear both he and his good friend Raymond Soulier were in love. While this identification is not borne out by any evidence, the costume of the sitter would support a date for the execution of the drawing in the early 1820's. She forcibly engages the attention of the spectator who feels himself in the presence of a real personality. Soulier, who had studied in England, instructed Delacroix in watercolor painting, the medium of the present drawing.

Provenance: P. A. Cheramy; Richard Goetz.

Bibliography: Raymond Escholier, *Delacroix, peintre, graveur, écrivain*, I, Paris, 1926, p. 79, repr; Mahonri Sharp Young, "Treasures in Gramercy Park," *Apollo*, LXXXV, 1967, p. 181.

GUSTAVE COURBET

ORNANS, DOUBS 1819 - LA TOUR DE PEILZ, SWITZERLAND 1877

6 "ANATOLE"

Black chalk, stumped. 9¾ x 8 inches.
Inscribed by the artist in black chalk at lower right: *a mon Viel ami Anatole/G. Courbet/69.*

It is not known whether the "Anatole" of the inscription refers to the man in this portrait or to the friend who was the recipient of the drawing, which Courbet drew in 1869. Most likely they were one and the same. As the artist was in Normandy for the most part between 1865 and 1869, painting sea pieces and landscapes, the rustic garb of the man portrayed here may be that of a Norman peasant or it may belie his actual calling. Courbet, a countryman himself, and his friends, Proudhon and Rochefort, were politically active in the cause of the common man which was to lead to their banishment two years later after the uprising of the Paris Commune.

Provenance: Private collection, London.

THEODORE CHASSERIAU

SANTA BARBARA DE SAMANA 1819 - PARIS 1856

7 LOUIS MARCOTTE DE QUIVIERES

Pencil. 13 x 9¾ inches.

Inscribed by the artist in pencil at lower right: *A mon ami Marcotte / Th. Chassériau 1841.*

In this carefully worked likeness of Louis Marcotte de Quivières, done in 1841 when the artist was twenty-two years old, Chassériau shows himself most adept in the Ingres tradition of pencil portraiture. The drawing remained in the family for several generations, and the identity of the sitter is indicated by labels attached at the back and presumably written by M. Marcotte de Quivières' son and grandson. At the same time, Chassériau also drew Mme Marcotte de Quivières (see Chevillard, no. 307). M. Marcotte de Quivières was apparently one of Chassériau's important patrons for he owned several drawings and at least three paintings, including the *Venus Anadyomene,* now in the Louvre, which caused such a sensation in the Salon of 1839.

Provenance: Louis Marcotte de Quivières and descendants.

Bibliography: Valbert Chevillard, *Peintre Romantique, Théodore Chassériau,* Paris, 1893, p. 307, no. 308; Mahonri Sharp Young, "Treasures in Gramercy Park," *Apollo,* LXXXV, 1967, p. 181.

DANTE GABRIEL ROSSETTI

LONDON 1828 - BIRCHINGTON-ON-SEA 1882

8 ELIZA HARRIET POLIDORI, THE ARTIST'S AUNT

Pencil. 9 x 7 inches.

Signed with monogram and dated at lower left: *1858.*

These firm features are those of Eliza Harriet Polidori, sympathetically set down by her nephew and godson, the Pre-Raphaelite painter and poet. His mother's youngest sister, she was the devoted spinster daughter who attended her mother until her death in 1853, and then in 1854 gave herself to further service as a member of the hospital unit which accompanied Florence Nightingale to the Crimea. As the young Dante Gabriel's godmother, she dutifully sent him advice and an occasional shilling, and he in turn dispatched some of his drawings to her, with the comment, "Excuse me if I have not done a landscape, as I am not capable of it. I have done a ship as you desire and two or three men on horseback" (Letter of January 16, 1839. See *Letters of Dante Gabriel Rossetti*, ed. by O. Doughty and J. F. Wahl, Oxford, 1965, p. 3).

Provenance: L. G. Duke.

SIR JOHN EVERETT MILLAIS

SOUTHAMPTON 1829 - LONDON 1896

9 MAN IN A TOP HAT

Pen and brown ink. 6½ x 7 inches.
Signed with initials and dated at lower left: *J. M. / 1882.*

The identity of the dignified Edwardian gentleman Millais drew with such a sure pen remains to be revealed, but there is no doubt that he was an important personage. The portrait, set within the loosely indicated medallion, was perhaps meant to be translated into engraving and used as a frontispiece or book illustration. It has been tentatively suggested that the subject was Sir Sidney Colvin, the distinguished keeper of the Department of Prints and Drawings at the British Museum (1884–1912), but in 1882 he was only thirty-seven and had not yet attained that post. The man in the portrait appears somewhat older and also more substantial in figure than Colvin.

Millais, at age nineteen one of the original Pre-Raphaelite triumvirate, turned increasingly to portraiture in his later work. He designed extensively for book illustration throughout most of his career.

Exhibitions: London, Maas Gallery, "The Pre-Raphaelites and their Contemporaries," 1961, no. 44.

ANSELM FEUERBACH

SPEYER 1829 - VENICE 1880

10 HEAD OF A MAN

Black and white chalk, gray wash, on brown paper. 12⅛ x 9¼ inches.
Verso: Drapery study. Signed with monogram in black chalk at lower left.

Feuerbach, member of a distinguished learned family, studied with Thomas Couture in Paris and afterwards traveled extensively in Italy to the end that his paintings reflect many influences. He was a skilled academic draughtsman who carefully prepared his paintings, largely devoted to historical and literary subjects. The drapery study on the verso of this sheet is typical of such preparation, but the well-modeled head of the melancholy young man on the recto seems to bear the individual stamp of portraiture.

Provenance: Dr. G. La Porte, New York (Lugt 1170).

Exhibitions: New York, The Drawing Shop, "The Non-Dissenters, Second Exhibition," 1963, no. 50.

CAMILLE JACOB PISSARRO

ISLAND OF SAINT-THOMAS 1830 - PARIS 1903

11 HEAD OF A BOY

Black and white chalk on blue-gray paper. 11¼ x 8½ inches.
Signed in black chalk at lower left: *C. Pissarro.* Stamped in gray-black ink at lower right and on verso: *C. P.* (Lugt 613e).
Verso: Black chalk study of girl asleep in a chair.

As the father of five sons, Pissarro was in a position to render the likeness of a small boy with warmth and understanding, and certainly he did not lack for models. This appealing study has been thought, perhaps wishfully, to represent the artist's eldest son Lucien, who became a painter and along with his father was converted to Neo-Impressionism for a period before he moved to England. Pissarro was the oldest and most devoted of the original group of Impressionist painters, and the only one to participate in all eight of their exhibitions from 1874 to 1886.

PAUL-GUSTAVE-LOUIS-CHRISTOPHE DORE

STRASBOURG 1832 - PARIS 1883

12 SEATED LADY

Pencil, brush and black ink with a few passages in pen and black ink, heightened with white, on a buff prepared ground, on boxwood. 1 10/16 x 1 11/16 inches.
Signed at lower right: *G. Doré.*

The woman seated here in quiet composure is possibly the artist's mother with whom Doré lived until her death, just two years before his own. They resided on the Rue St. Dominique, St. Germain, Paris, in a wonderful apartment "filled with artistic objects and mementoes of every sort . . . bits of armor, pictures, engravings, books, bric-a-brac, musical instruments, tapestry, curious weapons, china, souvenirs, several small dogs — whatever in short may lead to picturesqueness and comfort." Doré, famous and prosperous as a book illustrator, was used to laying out his designs in pen and pencil on blocks of wood that were later cut out for printing purposes by his numerous expert collaborators. This delicately worked drawing on boxwood, minute and precious, was however clearly not intended for the wood graver's tool.

Exhibitions: New York, Shepherd Gallery, "The Non-Dissenters IV," 1968, no. 155, pl. xv.

SIR EDWARD COLEY BURNE-JONES

BIRMINGHAM 1833 - LONDON 1898

13 STUDIES OF A BOY'S HEAD

Pencil. 8¼ x 6¾ inches.

The comely child studied on this page has been plausibly identified as the artist's son Philip, who was born in 1861 and grew up to become an artist. If the label affixed to the back of the mount is correct, he is shown at the age of fourteen and the drawing was therefore done in 1875. He appears at the age of twenty-three — although again deceptively younger in appearance than his actual age — in *The Artist's Family*, a painting dated 1884, owned by Graham McInnes, great-grandson of the artist (repr. Indianapolis, Herron Museum of Art, "The Pre-Raphaelites," 1964, no. 26). A protégé of Dante Gabriel Rossetti and a younger member of the Pre-Raphaelite movement, Burne-Jones was a prolific draughtsman who did not consistently achieve the quality manifest in this drawing. It carries an alternate traditional title *The Greek Boy*.

14 STUDIES FOR *ANDROMEDA*

Black and white chalk on brown paper. 13¼ x 19¾ inches.

Burne-Jones had already been experimenting with the illustration of the Perseus and Andromeda legend, when in 1875 the British statesman Arthur James Balfour commissioned a set of paintings on that theme for the decoration of the drawing room of his house in Carlton Gardens, London. Although work on the project spread out over more than a decade, it was never completed. Eight of the ten or eleven scenes originally planned are now in the Huntington Hartford Collection, New York. The heads of the Sonnenberg drawing, when the sheet is held vertically, are seen to be studies for the head of Andromeda in the Hartford panel entitled *The Rock of Doom*, dated 1884 – 88. The figure stands chained to a narrow rocky column, looking toward her liberator, her face turned in profile, almost identical with the head to the left of the drawing (or the lower head if the sheet is oriented vertically).

JAMES ABBOTT McNEILL WHISTLER

LOWELL, MASSACHUSETTS 1834 - LONDON 1903

15 SELF-PORTRAIT

Black chalk on brown paper. 7 x 5½ inches.

During one period of his life, Whistler reported that he made a practice of drawing his own portrait each night before going to bed. While one may suspect him of exaggeration, at least three chalk drawings, six in pen and ink, and eight in pencil apparently belong to this phase (see A. E. Gallatin, *Portraits of Whistler, A Critical Study and an Iconography*, New York, 1918). Whistler's pose here is identical to that in the chalk drawing in the Freer Gallery of Art, Washington, D.C. (Gallatin, no. 10), where it is more obvious that the artist inclines his head slightly forward as if to scrutinize his features.

Provenance: Alphonse W. Thibaudeau, Paris and London; John Postle Heseltine, London; Lord Leverhulme (sale, New York, The Anderson Galleries, 1926, no. 354, repr.); Robert Lehman, New York.

Bibliography: Elisabeth Luther Cary, *The Works of James McNeill Whistler*, New York, 1907, p. 196, no. 256.

Exhibitions: Paris, Palais des Beaux-Arts, *Catalogue of the Whistler Memorial Exhibition*, 1905, p. 67, no. 123 (according to E. L. Cary).

HILAIRE-GERMAIN-EDGAR DEGAS

PARIS 1834 - PARIS 1917

16 MARGUERITE DEGAS, LATER MME HENRI FEVRE 1842-1895

Black chalk and pencil. 10¼ x 8¾ inches. Stamped in red: *degas* (Lugt 658).

In his earlier years, Degas drew a number of independent portraits of both his immediate family in Paris and his relatives in Italy. The serious, sweet-faced young woman gently portrayed here was his younger sister who married the architect Henri Fevre in 1865. She was twenty-three at the time and she must have been near this age when her brother made this drawing. Earlier, in 1854, he had drawn her at the time of her first communion, and he later portrayed her twice in the picture *La Répétition de chant*, Dumbarton Oaks Collection, Washington, D.C.

Provenance: Paris, Galerie Georges Petit, "Vente Atelier Degas," Dec. 11 – 13, 1918, no. 240.

Bibliography: Mahonri Sharp Young, "Treasures in Gramercy Park," *Apollo*, LXXXV, 1967, p. 173, fig. 3.

PAUL CEZANNE

AIX-EN-PROVENCE 1839 - AIX-EN-PROVENCE 1906

17 TWO STUDIES OF MME CEZANNE, AND M. CHOCQUET

Pencil. 7¾ x 9⅛ inches.
Inscribed by the artist in pencil at left: + *tel*; at right: + *tel.*
Verso: Teapot and head of the artist's small son.

The larger part of this full study sheet, usually regarded as having been executed about 1877, is taken up by the two sketches of Mme Cézanne. At this time she was, in fact, not legally the artist's wife although she had lived with him since 1870 and had borne him a son in 1872. Their relationship had been concealed from Cézanne's difficult father, who, when he finally learned of it in 1878 and was confronted by his son's fearful denial of the situation, promptly halved his allowance with the remark that it should suffice for a bachelor. Ultimately, however, on April 28, 1886, the two were married in the presence of Cézanne's parents. Mme Cézanne, born Hortense Fiquet, had been a model and she was variously drawn and painted by her husband, always serious and sober in mien. The present sketch of her sewing is associated with a painting where she is shown similiarly occupied, but oriented to the right (Venturi no. 291).

The male head is a likeness of Victor Chocquet, the customs official who modestly but passionately collected modern paintings and got to know many of the artists whose work he admired and bought. Cézanne painted him several times as did Renoir.

Provenance: Lord Clark of Saltwood.

Bibliography: Lionello Venturi, *Cézanne, son art–son oeuvre*, Paris, 1936, I, no. 1240, II, pl. 343, no. 1240; Mahonri Sharp Young, "Treasures in Gramercy Park," *Apollo*; LXXXV, 1967, p. 181, fig. 13; Wayne V. Andersen, "Cézanne, Tanguy, Chocquet," *Art Bulletin*, 49, 1967, pp. 137–39, fig. 7; Wayne Andersen, *Cézanne's Portrait Drawings*, Cambridge, Mass., and London, 1970, pp. 19, 20, 75 (no. 33, repr.), 120 (verso: no. 99, repr.), 197 (Chocquet: no. 212, repr.).

18 SELF-PORTRAIT

Black chalk, stumped. 6⅞ x 5 inches.

Cézanne studied his own countenance on numerous occasions, both in drawings and in paintings. This portrait is dated by Professor Wayne V. Andersen as a work of about 1876–77. Shortly after it was executed, Cézanne's small son is thought to have penciled in a pair of spectacles and a lock of hair. In the removal of these childish additions in 1962, the drawing lost its freshness. The illustration in the *Burlington Magazine* of September, 1966, shows the drawing before treatment.

Provenance: Jean-Pierre Cézanne (grandson of the artist).

Bibliography: Wayne V. Andersen, "Two Unpublished Cézanne Self-portrait Drawings," *Burlington Magazine*, CVIII, 1966, p. 478, fig. 51; Mahonri Sharp Young, "Treasures in Gramercy Park," *Apollo*, LXXXV, 1967, p. 181; Wayne V. Andersen, *Cézanne's Portrait Drawings*, Cambridge, Mass., and London, 1970, pp. 21, 51, no. 4, repr.

SIMEON SOLOMON

LONDON 1840 - LONDON 1905

19 BEARDED MAN

Black chalk, stumped. Signed with monogram and dated at lower left: *SS / 6 11 61.*

This haunting representation of a melancholy bearded Hebrew, done in 1861 when the artist, himself an orthodox Jew, was only twenty-one, gives evidence of the promise of the precocious Solomon's gifts. In the following decade, however, he became a chronic alcoholic and eventually sank to the role of a sidewalk artist in Bayswater and the production of inconsequential sanguine drawings of heads when he was not selling shoelaces or matches. A peripheral figure on the Pre-Raphaelite scene, he was at one time close to Swinburne, who published an essay on his work in 1871, but later denounced him.

Exhibitions: London, The Maas Gallery, "The Pre-Raphaelites and their Contemporaries," 1961, no. 105.

BERTHE-MARIE-PAULINE MORISOT

BOURGES 1841 - PARIS 1895

20 WOMAN DRESSING HER HAIR

Red chalk. 11½ x 8½ inches.
Signed in red chalk at lower center: *Berthe Morisot.*

The poet and critic Paul Valéry, husband of a niece of the artist, characterized the work of Berthe Morisot as the diary of a woman who expressed herself in color and drawing, and such a drawing as this may be regarded as a charming entry in the journal of her daily life. One has the feeling that the subject must have been a member of her family or household rather than a professional model. Morisot, the sister-in-law of Manet, was the first woman painter to join the ranks of the Impressionists.

MARY CASSATT

PITTSBURGH 1844 - MESNIL-THERIBUS, OISE, FRANCE 1926

21 VERNON LEE (Violet Paget), 1895. 1856 - 1935

Watercolor over pencil and red chalk, on tan paper. 9½ x 6¾ inches.
Signed in pencil at lower right: *Mary Cassatt.*

The essayist and novelist Violet Paget, who used the pen name Vernon Lee, was a well-known personality of the English colony in Florence, noted for her brilliant conversation and caustic repartee. She wrote on aesthetics, politics, and Italian art and life, producing in addition several volumes of fiction. The best known of her seven books of travel essays is *Genius Loci: Notes on Places*, 1889.

This lively sketch was presumably made when she visited Mary Cassatt in July, 1895, at Mesnil-Théribus. She wrote of the artist: "Miss Cassatt is very nice, simple, an odd mixture of a self-recognizing artist, with passionate appreciation in literature, and the almost childish garrulous American provincial." Of herself, she wrote to her executor: "I absolutely prohibit any biography of me. My life is my own and I leave that to nobody." Vernon Lee's biography has nevertheless been written by Peter Gunn (1965). Her private papers and correspondence are preserved in the Colby College Library, Waterville, Maine, with the restriction that the letters are not to be published before 1980.

Bibliography: Adelyn Dohme Breeskin, *Mary Cassatt: A Catalogue Raisonné of the Oils, Pastels, Watercolors, and Drawings*, Washington, D.C., 1970, no. 625.

Exhibitions: Washington, D.C., National Gallery of Art, "Mary Cassatt, 1844–1926," 1970, no. 78, repr.

GIOVANNI BOLDINI

FERRARA 1845 - PARIS 1931

22 JACQUES-EMILE BLANCHE. 1861 - 1942

Pencil. 10⅜ x 7⅞ inches (sight).
Signed and dated in pencil at center right: *à J. Blanche / Boldini / Londres 9 8bre / 1884.*

Boldini's unusually direct portrait drawing shows the French painter and writer Blanche as an affluent young man in his early twenties. The son of a famous physician, Blanche went everywhere and knew everybody, not only in Paris, but also in London, including such diverse personalities as Edith Wharton and Jean Cocteau, whose portrait he painted on several occasions. His memoirs, published under the title *Cahiers d'un Artitste,* give an interesting picture of the artistic and literary life of the period. Francis Steegmuller in his recent biography of Cocteau notes that Blanche, "sharp-tongued and reportedly eunochoid, . . . was dubbed 'le vipère sans queue.' "

The fashionable portrait painter Boldini, who studied at the Academy in Florence, gained prominence first in London and then in Paris. He has been aptly characterized as the Italian equivalent of John Singer Sargent. Ferrara has devoted a museum to the work of this successful native son.

23 EDGAR DEGAS. 1834-1917

Black chalk on thin cream-colored paper. 10½ x 7½ inches.
Signed with initial and dated at lower center: *1883 / B.*

While it is obvious that Blanche and Biron formally sat to Boldini for their portraits (nos. 22 and 24), it seems unlikely that Degas was aware that his likeness was being taken by his Italian friend. Thin and intense, he appears tête-à-tête with an amused companion across a narrow café table (at the Nouvelle Athènes or the Café de la Rochefoucauld?), eyes glinting as he savors what was probably his own sardonic sally. The animation of the moment and the character of the man are remarkably fixed in this quick notation that could have served to illustrate the description of Degas by another of his friends, P. Plafond, who wrote in his biography: "A high, broad and domed forehead crowned with silky, chestnut hair, with quick, shrewd, questioning eyes deep-set under high arched eyebrows shaped like a circumflex, a slightly turned-up nose with wide nostrils, a delicate mouth half hidden under a small mustache." The slightly tousled hair and casually worn clothes are apposite to the remarks of George Moore (*Burlington Magazine*, XXXII, January, 1918, p. 28): "Not in his dress nor in his manner will you note anything glaringly distinctive, but for those who know him the suit of pepper-and-salt and the blue necktie tied round a loose collar are full of *him*."

Degas in his turn made two portraits of Boldini, whom he once described as a "monstre de talents."

Exhibitions: Poughkeepsie, New York, Vassar College, "Drawings and Watercolors from Alumnae and Their Families," 1961, no. 90, repr.

24 LE MARQUIS DE BIRON

Black chalk. 14½ x 9¾ inches.
Inscribed in pen and black ink on back of frame: *mon portrait au crayon par Boldini (1904) / au meilleur de mes amis Marcel Higuette, souvenir / de profonde et reconnaissante / affection / Berne 21 Février 1924 / Biron.*

As the late Frits Lugt remarked to Mr. J. Byam Shaw, the Marquis de Biron admired Boldini as an artist, and was himself, as a member of an ancient and distinguished French family, a suitable subject for the painter's portrait roster of the élite. A short, stocky man, the somewhat eccentric bachelor marquis was a gourmet and owner of fine vineyards in the Bordeaux country where the family seat is located. Otherwise, he lived with Spartan frugality and Mr. Germain Seligman in his *Merchants of Art*, 1961, noted that he was wont to wear "at least three topcoats and a heavy muffler wound about his neck, the whole topped by a bowler hat," rather than heat his frigid apartment on the rue d'Aguesseau, Paris.

A discriminating *marchand amateur*, who spent the last years of his life in Geneva, he owned an especially fine series of drawings and oil sketches by the Tiepolos and Guardi, many of which were acquired by the Metropolitan Museum of Art in 1937; others came into the possession of Biron's nephew, the late Duc de Talleyrand. Mr. Byam Shaw's account of the Biron drawings at the Metropolitan Museum appears in the Museum's *Journal*, III, 1970.

Provenance: Marquise de Biron; Marcel Higuette.

WALTER GREAVES

LONDON 1846 - LONDON 1930

25 THOMAS CARLYLE. 1795 - 1891

Point of brush and black wash over pencil, on buff paper. 10 x 11¾ inches.
Signed and dated in brush and black ink at upper left: *W. Greaves / 1871.*

The appearance of crusty Thomas Carlyle, the great British historian and man of letters, is best-known from the portrait that Whistler painted of him, *Arrangement in Grey and Black, No. 2.* It is interesting in this connection that Walter Greaves, the author of the present portrait, was, together with his brother Henry, for many years Whistler's student and assistant. He emulated his famous teacher even to the extent of trying to imitate the latter's appearance. Greaves painted Carlyle, his friend and neighbor in the Chelsea district of London, in 1872, a year after this study was made. Of portraiture, Carlyle remarked: "Often I have found a portrait superior in real instruction to half a dozen biographies."

Exhibitions: New York, Wildenstein, "From Realism to Symbolism: Whistler and His World," catalogue prepared by the Department of Art History and Archaeology, Columbia University, 1971, no. 72 (a full discussion of the portrait and its date).

PAUL GAUGUIN

PARIS 1848 - ATUANA, MARQUESAS ISLANDS 1903

26 MAN IN A SKULLCAP AND HEAD OF MIMI

Brush and black wash, black chalk. 6 x 7⅜ inches.

Of the three trips Gauguin made to Brittany between 1886 and 1890, the third sojourn from April, 1889, to November, 1890, was the longest and most important. He went first to Pont-Aven, but in June, annoyed by the presence of too many "abominable foreigners," moved with his friend Meyer de Haan and several other of his painter companions a few miles away to Le Pouldu. From there, he wrote to his wife Mette, "I'm on the seacoast in a fishermen's inn near a village of 150 people. I live like a peasant and have the name of a savage and I work every day in canvas trousers, all I have left." The owner of the inn was "Marie Poupée" or Mlle Marie Henry, who amiably permitted the artists to decorate the main room of the inn, even to the window panes, and who had a daughter Ida by Meyer de Haan. It is, however, her older daughter Léa, nicknamed Mimi, the child of an earlier liaison, whom Gauguin sketched in her Breton cap at the left of the Sonnenberg sheet, perhaps in nostalgic recollection of his own five children whom he had not seen for several years. Who the bearded man in the skullcap is remains to be discovered. When Léa's estate was auctioned off at the Hôtel Drouot, Paris, on March 16, 1959, this drawing and a gouache study of Mimi with a cat were among her effects (the gouache is repr. Jean Leymarie, *Paul Gauguin . . .*, London, 1961, p. 13).

Provenance: Marie Henry (later Mme Mothère), Le Pouldu, and her daughter, Léa (sale, Paris, Hôtel Drouot, March 16, 1959, no. 111).

Exhibitions: London, Marlborough Galleries, "XIX and XX Century European Masters," 1959, no. 24, repr.

VINCENT WILLEM VAN GOGH

GROOT-ZUNDERT 1853 - AUVERS-SUR-OISE, FRANCE 1890

27 MAN STANDING, HAT IN HAND

Pencil. 19¼ x 9¼ inches.

Van Gogh's letters, written to his brother Theo from The Hague in the autumn of 1882, comment repeatedly on the drawings of the aged residents of the almshouse on which he was at work. The orphan men, "as these poor old fellows from the workhouse are popularly called here," inspired a moving series of powerful studies reflecting the Dutch artist's compassion for humanity, particularly its less fortunate members. He could have been speaking of the Sonnenberg "orphan man" when he wrote, "He wears a large old overcoat, which gives him a curiously broad figure; I think you would enjoy this collection of almshouse men in their Sunday and everyday clothes. I also drew him sitting with a pipe." Elsewhere, Van Gogh, who writes of visiting the almshouse on Sunday, also makes mention of "the old fashioned hat," suggesting that the aged man was portrayed in his Sunday best, clutching the high hat that was a cherished relic of better days.

Provenance: Dr. H. P. Bremmer, The Hague; Dr. H. A. D. Thomas, Amsterdam.

Bibliography: J. B. de la Faille, *The Works of Vincent van Gogh, His Paintings and Drawings,* revised edition, Amsterdam, 1970, p. 356, no. F 953.

JOHN SINGER SARGENT

FLORENCE 1856 - LONDON 1925

28 AUGUSTUS SAINT-GAUDENS. 1848-1907

Charcoal. 23½ x 18½ inches.
Inscribed and signed by the artist at lower left: *To McKim John S. Sargent.*

Sargent and Saint-Gaudens, who had known each other since their student days in Paris, shared the lifelong friendship of Charles Follen McKim. McKim arranged commissions for both artists. He and his partner, Stanford White, who designed the bases for most of Saint-Gaudens' pieces, worked so closely with the sculptor that they often referred to themselves as "The Three Redheads." In 1890 McKim and White, who were in charge of the building and decoration of the Boston Public Library, invited the participation of Sargent and Saint-Gaudens. Sargent was engaged to do the murals for the upper staircase and Saint-Gaudens was to do a whole series of sculptures. The project went on for some years – the sculptures were unfinished at Saint-Gaudens' death in 1907 – and in January, 1900, the sculptor stopped in London on his way back from Paris to see how Sargent's designs were progressing. It may have been at this time that the present sketch was made. Although Sargent had painted a portrait of Mrs. Saint-Gaudens and her son in 1889 – the same year that the sculptor made reliefs of both Sargent and his sister Violet – Saint-Gaudens looks too old in the Sonnenberg drawing for it to have been executed at this time. His appearance here approximates that in E. G. E. Rand's portrait painted in 1904 (Metropolitan Museum) and is strikingly close to a formal photograph by De Witt C. Ward, taken in 1905 (see Louise Hall Thorp, *Saint-Gaudens and the Gilded Era*, Boston, 1969, repr. opp. p. 365).

29 ETHEL BARRYMORE. 1879-1959

Soft black pencil. 14 x 9⅜ inches.

Inscribed and signed by the artist at lower left: *To Mrs. Sears / from her friend / John S. Sargent.*

When both he and Ethel Barrymore were in Boston in 1903, Sargent wrote to the lovely young actress asking her to sit for him. Miss Barrymore, already a star, was appearing in *A Country Mouse*; Sargent had just returned to America to supervise the installation of some of his panels at the Boston Public Library. She sat to the artist at Mrs. Montgomery Sears' house where Sargent was a guest. Later, in her *Autobiography*, Miss Barrymore gave this amusing account of Sargent's working method: "He was delightful, humming around the room while he worked. He would sit down occasionally while in the midst of the drawing and play little snatches on the piano and then come back to work again." Despite these diversions, Sargent completed two drawings that day. The finished version he gave to Miss Barrymore and the first study, now in the Sonnenberg collection, he presented to his hostess.

Provenance: J. M. Sears, Boston; Mrs. J. D. C. Bradley.

Exhibitions: Boston, The Copley Society, "Portraits by Living Painters," 1914; New York, Portraits Inc., "Portraits of Personalities, Past and Present," 1958, no. 42; New York, M. Knoedler and Company, "Great Master Drawings of Seven Centuries," 1959, no. 86, pl. LV; New York, Portraits Inc., "Portrait Drawings 1900-1966," 1966, no. 86.

MAXIMILIEN LUCE

PARIS 1858 - PARIS 1941

30 PAUL SIGNAC. 1863-1935

Black chalk and a little blue chalk. 8 x 7 inches.

Inscribed by the artist in pencil: *a M. Ter - / Luce en souvenir de / Signac.*

The painter Signac, enthusiastic follower of Seurat, was the chief publicist of the artists grouped on the basis of their theories of divided color and dotted facture under the label of Neo-Impressionism. His work *D'Eugène Delacroix au Néo-Impressionnisme*, first published in *La Revue blanche* in 1898, was a kind of manifesto of the movement. This incisive profile portrait by a less well-known member of the group (see no. 35) does not emphasize the ebullient side of Signac's character, but it does make credible the report that the painter, an energetic yachtsman and sportsman, once said to a friend, only half in jest, "If you want to keep fit, get in a rage every morning for a quarter of an hour. It's as good as any gymnastics."

31 HENRY E. CROSS. 1856-1910

Black chalk. 8 x 6½ inches.

Luce's appealing portrayal of this major figure among the Neo-Impressionists is perhaps more revealing of the character of the subject than his profile study of Signac (no. 31). The sensitivity and charm of this cultivated painter clearly inspired the best effort of the draughtsman. Cross, who was born Delacroix but chose to use its English equivalent, was with Seurat and Signac a participant in the first *Salon des Indépendants* in 1884. An intimate friend of Signac, he eventually settled at Saint-Clair not too far from the former's villa at Saint-Tropez, and aided Signac in the preparation of his *D'Eugène Delacroix au Néo-Impressionnisme*, 1898, by translating Ruskin's *Elements of Drawing* for him. Luce's portrait of Cross has been dated about 1890, the year in which Luce — and perhaps Cross — was Signac's guest at Herblay. There is a painted portrait of Cross by Luce in the Musée National de l'Art Moderne, Paris.

Luce, who seems to have enjoyed portraying his Neo-Impressionist associates, also drew Seurat and Pissarro. For his own likeness, see no. 35.

Provenance: Robert Lehman, New York.

Bibliography: John Rewald, *Post-Impressionism from Van Gogh to Gauguin*, New York, 1956, p. 146, repr.

THEOPHILE-ALEXANDRE STEINLEN

LAUSANNE 1859 - PARIS 1923

32 CLAUDE DEBUSSY. 1862-1918

Black chalk. 14 x 10¼ inches.
Stamped in black ink at lower right: *St.*

"In his unrelenting gaze the pupils of his eyes seemed momentarily to dart from one spot to another like those of prey hypnotized by their own searching intensity." Colette's description is reflected in Steinlen's frontal portrait of Debussy. This flattering likeness minimizes the prominent brow which the great composer was always at pains to conceal. The combination of bulging forehead and Renaissance-type beard led his contemporaries to dub him "Le Christ hydrocéphalique." In addition to his genius as a composer, Debussy was one of the major music critics in his day, serving in this capacity with the Symbolist magazine, *La Revue blanche* (see no. 38). His appearance in Mr. Sonnenberg's drawing is very close to that in the portrait Jacques-Emile Blanche (see no. 22) painted in 1902, the year that saw the première of the composer's opera, *Pelléas et Mélisande.*

GEORGES-PIERRE SEURAT

PARIS 1859 - PARIS 1891

33 MME APPERT AND MME SEURAT

Conté crayon. 12⅝ x 9½ inches.

More often than not, Seurat used members of his family as models for the impersonal figures of his drawings and paintings, and the tradition handed down with this beautiful drawing identifies the closed silhouettes of the two women *en promenade* as those of his mother and sister. Honed and polished as the images are in terms of their refined abstraction, they do still seem to retain an aura of individuality that lends support to the tradition that descended to Mme Fernand Canu, a second cousin. In the tall, slender form in three-quarter view on the left, one presumably recognizes Mme Léon Appert, Seurat's sister Marie-Berthe, his elder by twelve years and often the recipient of his drawings and paintings. She turns with a hint of graceful deference to the fuller figure of an older woman seen squarely from the back, her shoulders ever so slightly bowed with the sixty or so years that would have been Mme Seurat's in 1881 – 82 when the drawing was probably made. An independent work with no connection to a painting, the drawing stands at the beginning of what has been termed the artist's maturity, which began at age twenty-one or -two and ended a decade later with his death in 1891. It was listed in the inventory of 1891 as no. 108.

Provenance: The Seurat family, including Mme Fernand Canu.

Bibliography: C. M. De Hauke, *Seurat et son oeuvre*, II, Paris [1962], no. 506, repr.; Robert Herbert, *Seurat's Drawings*, New York, 1962, p. 165, pl. 141 and p. 187, no. 141; Mahonri Sharp Young, "Treasures in Gramercy Park," *Apollo*, LXXXV, 1967, pp. 178, 181, fig. 11.

WALTER RICHARD SICKERT

MUNICH 1860 - BATHAMPTON, SOMERSET 1942

34 SIR MAX BEERBOHM. 1872 - 1956

Pencil on thin cream paper. 10 x 8 inches.

By filling, even crowding the page with the noticeably large, round head and one small, slender hand, Sickert effectively dramatized the most distinctive aspects of the person of the English writer and caricaturist. The "incomparable Max," as he was characterized by George Bernard Shaw, appears on the verge of giving expression to one of the witticisms that made his talks on the British radio so popular from 1935 on. A well-known figure in the London of the *décadents* and the Gay Nineties, he retired in middle age to Rapallo, Italy (1910), but continued to write. His best-known work is *Zuleika Dobson*, 1911, a satirical novel of Oxford undergraduate life. For one of his caricatures, see no. 39.

Sickert, the Munich-born artist who studied under Whistler and was much influenced by his friendship with Degas, was the most important of the English Impressionists. He founded the Camden Town Group (1911), which eventually became the London Group.

Provenance: Sale, London, Christie's, July 20, 1956, no. 25.

Exhibitions: Poughkeepsie, New York, Vassar College, "Drawings and Watercolors from Alumnae and Their Families," 1961, no. 102, repr.

PAUL SIGNAC

PARIS 1863 - PARIS 1935

35 MAXIMILIEN LUCE. 1858-1941

Black chalk. 10½ x 7⅝ inches.

Signed with monogram in pen and dark blue ink at lower right: *P.S.*

Luce, who joined the circle of the Neo-Impressionist painters around 1887 only to return eventually to an Impressionist manner, actively participated in the Anarchist-Communist politics to which the other members of the group subscribed in theory. Trained as an engraver at age fourteen and forced to earn his living as an illustrator as well as painter, he contributed illustrations to a variety of Anarchist journals, including *La Révolte*; in 1894, he was imprisoned for his political activities. During the later 1890's, he traveled and painted the terrible "Black Country" of Belgium where Van Gogh had lived.

As was noted under no. 31, Luce was the guest of Signac in 1890, at which time his host drew and dated a half-length portrait of him (repr. John Rewald, *Post-Impressionism*, New York, 1956, p. 141). Signac's placement of the head on the present sheet suggests that he may have originally intended a more extensive view of his model, who perhaps sat reading as Signac forcefully registered his somewhat undistinguished features in sequences of vigorous parallel hatchings. Mr. Sonnenberg also owns a second drawing of Luce by Signac.

Provenance: Félix Fénéon.

SIR FRANK BRANGWYN

BRUGES 1867 - DITCHLING, SUSSEX 1956

36 SELF-PORTRAIT

Black chalk. 7¼ x 5¼ inches.
Signed with initials in black chalk at lower right: *FB.*
Illegibly inscribed in pencil at lower right: *W de B coll.*

G. K. Chesterton described Brangwyn, the rugged Welshman whose talent was basically self-taught, as "the most masculine of all modern men of genius." After a brief interlude in the studio of William Morris, the youthful Brangwyn signed onto a ship as a cabin boy and began the travels which took him to Spain, the Middle East, Russia, and South Africa. Best-known for his large-scale murals – he did some for Radio City, New York – Brangwyn was considered by many to be among the finest draughtsmen of his day.

The changing aspect of his face is well-recorded in several drawings. The present portrait shows him as a man in his fifties or sixties, his dominant feature large observant eyes beneath pointed brows. The first living artist to be so honored, he was given a retrospective exhibition at Burlington House, London, in 1952. Two museums, one in Bruges and the other in Orange, France, are devoted to his work.

Provenance: Count William de Belleroche.

EDOUARD VUILLARD

CUISEAUX 1868 - LA BAULE 1940

37 PRINCESS MARTHE LAHOVARY BIBESCO. 1887-

Pastel on yellow-brown paper. 16 x 12 inches.
Signed in black chalk at lower right: *E. Vuillard.*

Born in Bucharest, the writer and novelist Princess Bibesco lived and wrote chiefly in France, both under her own name and the pseudonym Lucile Decaux. Among her works are the novel *Catherine-Paris,* 1927; *Noblesse de robe,* 1928, a description of the world of *la haute couture*; *Au bal avec Marcel Proust,* 1929; *Lettres d'une fille de Napoléon (1853–1859),* 1933, and *La Duchesse de Guermantes,* 1950.

Vuillard, a "tranquil artist" as Gide termed him, was a member of the Nabis with the nickname "le Zouave." Later as an exponent of *Intimisme,* he became known for his rendering of simple intimate interiors, and while he himself said, "I don't paint portraits. I paint people in their homes," this drawing is a charming example of his "pure" portraiture. According to a letter from her daughter, the Princess preferred this pastel among the several Vuillard made of her. Pastel was a favored medium of the artist.

Provenance: Walter Goetz.

38 THADEE NATANSON. 1868-1951

Pencil. 4¾ x 3¾ inches.

Signed with initials in pencil at lower right: *E. V.*

Thadée Natanson and his brothers Alexandre and Louis-Alfred were the founders of *La Revue blanche* (1891 - 1903), a literary and dramatic review of the Symbolist era. Vuillard, who was among its contributors, variously portrayed the brothers and their families, including a painting of the Thadée Natansons' salon at Villeneuve-sur-Yonne about 1897, a picture in the collection of the late Emil Bührle. Thadée was the first husband of Misia Sert, friend of Diaghilev and "queen of the Russian ballet," who was fifteen at the time of their marriage. Mr. Sonnenberg also owns a third Vuillard drawing, a portrait head of Mme Alexandre Natanson.

SIR HENRY MAXIMILIAN BEERBOHM

LONDON 1872 - RAPALLO, ITALY 1956

39 "JOSEPH CONRAD AND HIS CIRCLE." 1857-1924

Pencil and watercolor. 10 x 8 inches.

Inscribed by the artist in pencil at center right: *Frontispiece for / that dreadful work / "Joseph Conrad and / His Circle." / Max / 1935.* Drawn on a sheet of the artist's writing paper from the Villino Chiaro at Rapallo.

Joseph Conrad had been dead more than a decade when Beerbohm, living in retirement in Italy, was moved to produce this caricature of the celebrated author and his wife on a sheet of his letter paper. It embodied his pungent reaction to the publication of Jessie Conrad's book about her husband which appeared in 1935 under the title *Joseph Conrad and His Circle.* Beerbohm had liked and admired the author, but obviously not his wife nor her book. Such a drawing was probably made solely for the artist's own amusement or the entertainment of a friend.

Lady Ottoline Morrell (see no. 47), on meeting the Conrads, described the novelist as a "charming gentleman with high square shoulders which he shrugged now and again so lightly." Of his wife, she commented, "She seemed a nice and good-looking fat creature, an excellent cook." Mrs. Conrad also published *A Handbook of Cookery for a Small House,* 1923, a work Beerbohm perhaps found more commensurate with her talents.

Bibliography: Mahonri Sharp Young, "Treasures in Gramercy Park," *Apollo,* LXXXV, 1967, p. 171, repr.

FRANCIS DODD

HOLYHEAD, ANGLESEY 1874 - LONDON 1949

40 VIRGINIA WOOLF. 1882-1941

Charcoal on blue paper. 12 x 7½ inches.
Signed and dated in pencil at upper right: *Francis Dodd / 1908*; inscribed by the artist in pencil at lower center: *Miss V. Stephen*; inscribed in another hand in pencil at upper left: *Virginia Stephen.*

The eminent novelist and essayist, the "queen of Bloomsbury," was still Miss Virginia Stephen when Francis Dodd drew her at the age of twenty-six, four years before her marriage to Leonard Woolf. It was, in fact, just shortly afterward in February, 1909, that she and Lytton Strachey, the biographer, entered upon an engagement, mutually terminated, however, almost immediately. At this time she was already working on her first novel, *The Voyage Out*, although it was not to be published until 1915. Dodd shows her long, aquiline face still soft with the bloom of youth, but reserved and remote in its intelligence.

Dodd, the brother-in-law of Muirhead Bone, had just successfully established himself in London about this time after some years in Manchester. He was in touch with Miss Stephen some time before June 3, 1907, when she wrote, "Dodd, a little New English Club artist, half drunk and ecstatic, wishes to paint my portrait, and I am to sit in the afternoons from 2 to 4.30. Alone?" On August 10, 1908, however, it is about a print rather than a painting that she reports to her sister, "Dodd writes that he is much pleased with his print of me, & will send me a copy; it looked rather too stout, so he added two flounces to the dress. The only good part was the line of the skirt – so my vanity once more will be shocked." Dodd etched four plates of "Miss Stephen," two in 1908 and two the following year, and this 1908 drawing was, one supposes, made in the course of Dodd's preparations for one or the other of these portraits (see the *Print Collector's Quarterly*, XIII, 1926, p. 369). While none of the plates were available for comparison with the Sonnenberg drawing when the present catalogue was compiled, Mr. and Mrs. Quentin Bell, in correspondence, kindly reported that the drawing bears no resemblance to the etching in their possession, which shows Miss Stephen, standing, in profile to the left. (They also directed the compiler to the references to the sitting, which occur in the notable Virginia Woolf archive in the Berg Collection of the New York Public Library, kindly made available by Dr. Lola L. Szladits.)

Exhibitions: London, Maas Gallery, "Pre-Raphaelites to Post-Impressionists," 1965, no. 38.

41 SIR JACOB EPSTEIN. 1880-1959

Charcoal on blue paper. 12½ x 10¾ inches (sight).
Signed in pencil at center right: *Dodd.*
Inscribed in pencil at upper left: *Jacob Epstein, Sculptor 1910.*

This vigorous characterization of the vital young American-born sculptor shows him standing at his work table, mallet and chisel in hand, very much as he appears in Dodd's drypoint portrait dated 1909 (four states, twenty-three impressions). Were it not for the inscribed date 1910, one would assume that the drawing was undoubtedly preliminary to the print. Although the pose was altered in some respects in the print and the sculptor shown with a large block of stone on his work stand, drawing and drypoint are on the whole so similar that one cannot exclude the possibility that the date was added later in a lapse of memory on the part of the inscriber.

The English painter and etcher Dodd was among Epstein's first friends – Augustus John was another – when he arrived in London in 1905 following three years of study in Paris. It was Dodd who in 1907 was instrumental in Epstein's securing his first major commission, the sculptural decoration of the then new British Medical Association building in the Strand; the eighteen figures, which were the source of the first of the long series of Epstein controversies, are now destroyed. In 1911, the year of Dodd's marriage, Epstein executed a portrait head of his bride, possibly as a wedding gift. During the first years of World War I, Dodd, then engaged in producing a series of one hundred fifty portrait drawings of admirals and generals, put another commission in Epstein's way, a bust of Admiral Lord Fisher for the Duchess of Hamilton.

The young Epstein was also the subject of an etching by Augustus John, done about 1905-06.

Provenance: John Quinn.

Bibliography: *John Quinn Catalogue of Paintings, Watercolors, Drawings and Sculptures*, foreword by Forbes Watson, Huntington, N. Y., 1926, p. 17, repr. p. 140.

GWENDOLEN JOHN

TENBY, WALES 1876 - LONDON 1939

42 ARTHUR SYMONS. 1865-1945

Black chalk on buff paper. 10⅛ x 9¾ inches.
Stamped in black ink at lower right: *Gwen John.*

Symons, Welsh-born like Gwen John, was a critic and poet who did much to bring French and Italian literature to the notice of British readers. He is best-known for his early work,

The Symbolist Movement in Literature, 1899; his own poetry reflects the influence of the French *décadents* as did his life style. His translations included the works of Baudelaire and d'Annunzio.

Gwen John, painter sister of Augustus John (see no. 46), lived mostly in France where she was the friend of Rodin, Rilke, and the philosopher Maritain. Symons' thin, introverted countenance was an appropriate subject for her delicately probing pencil. The drawing was made in the early 1920's. Mr. Sonnenberg also owns another likeness of the critic by Gwen John; there he is shown with the book he is reading.

Provenance: Edwin John (nephew of the artist).

Bibliography: Mahonri Sharp Young, "Treasures in Gramercy Park," *Apollo*, LXXXV, 1967, p. 173.

Exhibitions: New York, Davis Galleries, "Gwen John," 1965, no. 33; London, Arts Council of Great Britain, "Gwen John Retrospective Exhibition," 1968, no. 99, repr.

BOARDMAN ROBINSON

SOMERSET, NOVA SCOTIA 1876 - STAMFORD, CONNECTICUT 1952

43 GEORGE BIDDLE. 1885-

Pen and black ink, gray wash. 9⅛ x 7⅞ inches.

Signed with initials at right center: *B R*; inscribed and dated by the artist at lower center: *George Biddle '37*.

In the winter of 1936–37, both George Biddle and Boardman Robinson were teaching at Colorado Springs Fine Arts Center, and when at that time the Arts Center published *Boardman Robinson: Ninety-Three Drawings*, 1937, Biddle provided an introduction that is still an important source for information on Robinson's life and career. Robinson's portrait of Biddle, which was made in the same year, accurately delineates the pointed, sensitive profile of his colleague, who had in 1936 already represented Robinson in a lithograph. That Robinson worked directly in pen without any preliminary pencil work witnesses the skill developed over his many years as a cartoonist and illustrator for various New York papers and periodicals before he turned to painting and became known for his mural decorations in the R.K.O. Building, New York, and the Department of Justice, Washington, D. C.

Biddle, a member of the well-known Philadelphia family, who passed the Pennsylvania bar before embarking on his long career as painter and lithographer, also supplied a mural for the Justice Building; he was active as a war artist in Africa and Italy, and has since traveled and worked in Tahiti and India. He has, as well, written extensively on art and the artist. For examples of his draughtsmanship, see nos. 54 and 55.

MARSDEN HARTLEY

LEWISTON, MAINE 1877 - ELLSWORTH, MAINE 1943

44 SELF-PORTRAIT

Black chalk. 12 x 9 inches.

Marsden Hartley sketched his own rugged features as economically and freely as he painted the rock-bound coast of his native state. However summary this self-portrait is, it does convey a sense of the dynamism of the man. A poet by avocation if not by profession, Hartley wrote about many of the things he painted. While three small collections of his verse were published in his lifetime—*Twenty-Five Poems*, 1925, *Androscoggin*, 1940, and *Sea Burial*, 1941—Hartley left five hundred more in manuscript at the time of his death. A selection made from these and the volumes already in print was published in 1945.

At least one other version of the self-portrait exists.

Provenance: Estate of the artist.

Exhibitions: Poughkeepsie, New York, Vassar College, "Drawings and Watercolors from Alumnae and Their Families," 1961, no. 111, repr.

RAOUL DUFY

LE HAVRE 1877 - PARIS 1953

45 ADOLPHE BASLER. 1876-1951

Black pencil. 22 x 15½ inches.

Signed and inscribed in pencil at lower right: *Raoul Dufy / [à?] Adolf Basler.*

The story goes that the young Raoul Dufy, alarmed by his precocious facility in drawing, stopped using his right hand and began to draw with his left to the end that, while he always remained ambidextrous, he came to use his right hand exclusively for writing and his left for drawing and painting.

This incredible dexterity was admired by Basler, the subject of this portrait that is so expressive in its minimal line. At the same time the well-known critic blamed it for the artist's failure to fulfill his talent. In *Modern French Painting: the Modernists from Matisse to Segonzac*, New York [1931], pp. 43 f., Basler remarked that "Dufy has never been able to set sail as did the other great 'Fauves,' such as Matisse and Derain. . . . His piquant and facile art . . . is to great painting what operetta is to opera. . . ." Basler, an influential figure in modern art, wrote numerous monographs and also appeared regularly in the pages of several magazines including *La Revue blanche* and *Le Mercure de France.*

Provenance: Alex Maguy.

SIR AUGUSTUS EDWIN JOHN

TENBY, WALES 1878 - LONDON 1961

46 SELF-PORTRAIT

Pencil on buff paper. 4¼ x 3¾ inches.

Augustus John, who as a painter is perhaps best known for his brilliant portraits, here drew his own youthful features with serious intensity. It was at this time that he was experimenting with etching, repeatedly delineating his own face very much in the manner of the young Rembrandt, and this drawing, done about 1901, is close enough to one of the etchings to be considered as a preparatory stage. The print, which exists in a single impression, was catalogued and illustrated by Campbell Dodgson in *A Catalogue of Etchings by Augustus John, 1901 – 1914*, London, 1920, no. 4.

A powerful, passionate personality, given on occasion to living and traveling like a gypsy, John was described by Wyndham Lewis (see no. 63) as "a great man of action into whose hands the fairies stuck a brush instead of a sword." When Lady Ottoline Morrell (see no. 47) sat to him eight years or so after he drew this small self-likeness, she wrote of his appearance: "His dark auburn hair was long and cut across the front like a fringe, and with a square beard, his curious pale face and sea-anemone eyes, he might have been a Macedonian king or a Renaissance poet."

Provenance: Mrs. Harold Gilman (widow of the first president of the London Group of artists).

47 LADY OTTOLINE MORRELL. 1873-1938

Gouache over pencil. 11⅞ x 8⅜ inches.
Signed in pencil at lower right: *John.*

Lady Ottoline, daughter of Major-General Arthur Bentinck and wife of Philip Morrell, M.P., was a well-known hostess whose gatherings at Garsington Manor near Oxford were satirized in the novel *Crome Yellow*, 1922, by Aldous Huxley; she was also the model for Hermione Roddice in D. H. Lawrence's *Women in Love*, 1920. Bertrand Russell, whose autobiography records his liaison with her, described her thus:

> "Ottoline was very tall, with a long thin face something like a horse, and very beautiful hair of an unusual colour, more or less like that of marmalade, but rather darker. Kind ladies supposed it to be dyed, but in this they were mistaken. She had a very beautiful, gentle, vibrant voice, indomitable courage, and a will of iron." (*The Autobiography of Bertrand Russell, 1914-1944*, Boston, 1968, p. 316)

Lady Ottoline noted in her diary that she sat to Augustus John on numerous occasions in the spring of 1909, in Whistler's old studio at 8 Fitzroy Street, London, sometimes in her "dull violet velvet dress with green sleeves," sometimes in a "long, white dress." John's portrait was never finished but "many a drawing was done." (*Ottoline, The Early Memoirs of Lady Ottoline Morrell*, ed. by Robert Gathorne-Hardy, London, 1963, pp. 158, 163, 165).

Exhibitions: London, Reid and Lefevre, Ltd., "Augustus John," 1947; New York, Portraits, Inc., "Portrait Drawings 1900–1966," April 20–May 10, 1966, no. 71.

48 THE MARCHESA ORIGO. 1902-

Pencil. 19½ x 14 inches.
Signed in pencil at center right: *John.* Inscribed by the artist in pencil at lower left: *The Marchesa Origo.*

The Marchesa Origo, daughter of the American diplomat W. Bayard Cutting and Lady Sybil Cuffe, is a woman of letters who grew up in the Villa Medici near Florence and still lives in Italy. Her book *War in Val d'Orcia, A Diary*, 1947, is an account of her experiences there during World War II. Among her other works are *The Last Attachment: the Story of Byron and Teresa Guiccioli*, 1949; *The Merchant of Prato, Francesco di Marco Datini, 1335–1410*, 1957; *The World of San Bernardino*, 1963; and her autobiography, *Images and Shadows*, 1970.

Bibliography: Mahonri Sharp Young, "Treasures in Gramercy Park," *Apollo*, LXXXV, 1967, p. 173.

JOSEPH STELLA

MURO LUCANO, ITALY 1879 - NEW YORK 1946

49 ELLIS ISLAND STUDY: YOUNG COUPLE

Black chalk on tan paper. 27 x 22 inches.
Signed in black chalk at lower right: *Joseph Stella.*

Best known as an exponent of Futurism, Stella began his professional career as a magazine illustrator. In 1916 the magazine *Survey* published an *exposé* of conditions on Ellis Island accompanied by Stella's illustrations. The present drawing — one of the most impressive studies in this group — is carefully drawn with fastidious attention to details of feature and dress. The woman wears the starched headdress and laced bodice of her native Italy. She is recognizable in another sketch, this time gazing softly at her child (see Newark Museum, "Drawings of Joseph Stella from the Collection of Rabin & Krueger," 1962, no. 13, repr.). Stella, who received a doctor's education before he left Italy, drew many studies of immigrants in much poorer circumstances than his own.

Provenance: Estate of the artist.

Exhibitions: New York, Zabriskie Gallery, "Joseph Stella," 1958, no. 21.

AMEDEO MODIGLIANI

LIVORNO 1884 - PARIS 1920

50 M. KOHLER

Brush and black wash on buff paper. 17 x 11½ inches.

Inscribed by the artist in pencil at lower left: *à Kohler bien amicalement / Modigliani.*

Modigliani drew constantly throughout the short career that tuberculosis, complicated by alcoholism and drugs, ended at age thirty-six, and a sizable part of his *oeuvre* consists of drawings in the distinctive original style he evolved from elements of the art of Cézanne and Brancusi along with African sculpture. A great many of the drawings are portraits, always vertical in format and usually representing a single figure but rarely executed in brush as this one is. No information is forthcoming as to the identity of the slender, bearded man who probably posed for Modigliani several years after the young Italian artist arrived in Paris in 1906. There is a companion portrait of Mme Kohler, also boldly worked in brush and likewise bearing a friendly inscription to M. Kohler. It is reproduced by the artist's daughter in her book on her father as the pendant of the Sonnenberg drawing but without any indication of ownership. M. Kohler also appears in what seems to be an earlier variant sketch in the collection of Mrs. Sydney G. Biddle, West Chester, Pennsylvania (see Ambrogio Ceroni, *Amedeo Modigliani, dessins et sculptures*, Milan, 1965, no. 7, pl. 7). Could he have been Albert Kohler, a Swiss painter and sculptor of Modigliani's generation, who was in Paris between 1912 and 1914?

Bibliography: Jeanne Modigliani (trans. by Esther Rowland Clifford), *Modigliani, Man and Myth*, New York, 1958, pl. 80; Franco Russoli, *Modigliani, Drawings and Sketches*, New York, 1969, no. 4, repr.

Exhibitions: Paris, Galerie Charpentier, "Cent Tableaux de Modigliani," 1959.

51 MICHEL

Pen and brown ink. 16½ x 10 inches.

Signed in pencil at lower right: *Modigliani.* Inscribed by the artist in pen and brown ink at upper left, 1 *Anno*; at left center, *Michel*; at lower left, *ESSAIS*.

From 1914–15 on, it was not unusual for Modigliani, both in the painted portraits and in his drawings, to introduce the subject's name within the composition and occasionally to add a cryptic word or phrase like the "savoir" appearing in his portrait of Picasso or the "essais" used here. In portraits of his friends like the painter Moïse Kisling, who permitted him to share his studio, or Leopold Zborowski, the helpful bookseller who acted as his dealer, or the novelist Blaise Cendrars, he employed only the last name; but in other instances, he inscribed the first name alone and for the most part these personalities cannot be further identified. (The use of the full name is rare.) Michel's enigmatic visage, therefore, has remained anonymous but unforgettable in the sophisticated notation of the inordinately tiny eyes set like sequins above the sharp nose and faintly smiling lips.

The use of pen and ink is exceptional as Modigliani ordinarily preferred to draw with a pencil.

PERCY WYNDHAM LEWIS

BAY OF FUNDY 1884 - LONDON 1957

52 ROY CAMPBELL. 1901-1957

Pencil, brush and brown wash. 9⅜ x 7 inches.
Signed and inscribed by the artist in pencil at lower center: *Wyndham Lewis. 1936 / portrait of Roy Campbell.*

The South African poet first met Wyndham Lewis when he came to London in his teens, and he soon became a disciple and friend of the Vorticist artist-writer. He served as the model for several of Lewis's characters, including "Zulu" Blades in *The Apes of God*, 1930, one of Lewis's many controversial books. (Campbell's equally controversial review of *The Apes*, originally commissioned, then rejected by the *New Statesman*, was finally published in Lewis's own pamphlet *Satire and Fiction.*) In a letter to Mrs. Campbell in August, 1936, Lewis asked if the Campbells would sit for a "family group," when he visited them in Sussex the following week. As it turned out, no painting was undertaken but Lewis did at this time make several sketches of the poet and his wife, including this schematic yet expressive head.

Ranked by Dame Edith Sitwell as "one of the very few great poets of our time," Campbell was described in her autobiography *Taken Care Of*, 1965: "Of great stature, build, strength, and vitality, he had eyes of the flashing blue of the kingfisher. . . . He was never a fascist. But a deeply religious man, he fought against the Reds in Spain." The poet was killed in an automobile accident within a few months of Lewis's death.

53 MRS. WYNDHAM LEWIS

Pastel on blue paper. 19¼ x 12½ inches (sight).
Signed and dated in pencil at lower right: *Wyndham Lewis / 1940.*

This impersonal, rhythmically stylized portrait of the artist's wife was probably done in Canada or the United States where the Lewises spent the war years. As is often the case in Lewis's portraiture, the hands of the sitter play an important part in the composition, almost in competition with the face.

Gladys Anne Hoskyns, at one time an art student, married the artist in 1929 unbeknown to all but a few friends. Often a model for her husband, she was a devoted wife, particularly in the later years complicated by Lewis's illness and failing sight. Of "Froanna," Lewis wrote breezily to Mrs. John Rothenstein, in December, 1939, "You say you never know whether people are married or not. My wife and I were most orthodoxly spliced a long time ago. . . . She is a very good sort and I am sure you would like her. We have no children. She is a blonde, she tends to put on fat, . . . she has ridden all over the Atlas on a mule and is a great reader of my books: but you can see she is a wife in a thousand."

Provenance: Private collection, London.

GEORGE BIDDLE

PHILADELPHIA 1885 -

54 GEORGE SANTAYANA. 1863 - 1952

Pencil and charcoal. 13 x 9¾ inches.
Signed and dated in pencil at lower right: *George Biddle 1952;* inscribed by the artist in pencil at lower left: *George Santayana.*

Dated 1952, the year Santayana died, this drawing is very possibly the last likeness of the famous Spanish-born philosopher, who began his career as a poet and also wrote a successful novel, *The Last Puritan*, 1935. In his book, the *Yes and No of Contemporary Art*, 1957, the artist describes the occasion which the drawing no doubt commemorates. "During a recent year's stay in Rome I had the rare privilege of renewing an earlier and casual acquaintance with George Santayana. [Biddle is an alumnus of Harvard University where Santayana taught from 1907 to 1912.] In his somewhat shabby and overcrowded bedroom in the Convent of the Blue Nuns I listened with respectful and fascinated excitement to the brilliant, enigmatic and solitary philosopher.... Although he was in his eighty-ninth year, almost blind and deaf, and actually dying of stomach cancer, he radiated charm, kindly tolerance, humor and a friendly acceptance of life. . . . The last occasion on which I saw him, four months before his death, he told me he had been reading Ovid that morning." Biddle made two lithographs of Santayana, one based on this drawing but with the head reversed, and another in profile.

Exhibitions: New York, Cober Gallery, "George Biddle, Silverpoints," 1963, no. 17.

55 EDMUND WILSON. 1895 -

Charcoal. 13 x 11¼ inches.
Signed in pencil and dated at lower right: *George Biddle / October 1956.*

The well-known critic and man of letters is represented as he appeared in the middle 1950's, which saw the publication of one of his most widely-read essays, *The Scrolls from the Dead Sea*, 1955, and also *A Piece of My Mind: Reflections at 60*, 1956. In the latter work, he remarked, "My own generation in America has not had so gay a journey as we expected when we started out," a comment which seems to find reflection in his countenance. Among his more recent works are *The Cold War and the Income Tax*, 1963, recounting the difficulties he experienced when he failed to file his returns between 1946 and 1955, and criticizing the American scene, and *O Canada: An American's Notes on Canadian Culture*, 1965.

Exhibitions: New York, Cober Gallery, "George Biddle, Silverpoints," 1963, no. 10.

ROGER DE LA FRESNAYE

LE MANS 1885 - GRASSE 1925

56 SELF-PORTRAIT

Pen and black ink over pencil on dark cream paper. 8 1/16 x 4 13/16 inches.
Atelier stamp in black ink at lower right: *R de la Fresnaye.*

The short career of La Fresnaye, an artist influenced by Cézanne and at one point working in a somewhat refined Cubist mode, was shadowed by ill health. Near the end of World War I, he was invalided out of the service and retired to the south of France where he eventually died of tuberculosis. A sequence of self-portraits made in the last four or five years of his life charts the sad progress of his illness. This portrait, showing him in the cape he frequently wore, is placed at the beginning of the series when he was still in relatively fair health. Although definitely a self-likeness, it seems deliberately to avoid suggesting the handsome appearance of the artist, a prematurely white-haired man of elegance and refinement.

Provenance: Bondi-Jaray, London.

Bibliography: Germain Seligman, *Roger de La Fresnaye*, Paris, 1969, no. 610.

HENRI GAUDIER-BRZESKA

ST. JEAN DE BRAYE 1891 - NEUVILLE ST. VAAST 1915

57 EZRA POUND. 1885 -

Brush and black ink. 19½ x 14½ inches (sight).

The strong profile of the controversial poet lent itself admirably to Gaudier-Brzeska's bold, calligraphic simplification that fills the page like a giant ideograph. The resemblance, however, remains striking and unmistakable. The same is not true of the abstract marble head for which the present sheet was apparently one of a number of preliminary drawings made in 1914. Pound in *Gaudier-Brzeska, A Memoir*, 1916, calls it "Hieratic Head of Ezra

Pound," noting: "The bust of me was most striking, perhaps, two weeks before it was finished. I do not mean to say that it was better, it was perhaps a *kinesis*, whereas it is now a *stasis*." The drawing could be said to be even more in the nature of a *kinesis*. Another drawing of the same series, probably made prior to this one, is illustrated by Horace Brodsky, *Henri Gaudier-Brzeska, 1891–1915*, London, 1933, p. 61.

Poet and sculptor were both members of the English art movement known as Vorticism (Pound is credited by Wyndham Lewis [see no. 63] as so christening it); it faded out during the First World War, which also ended the career of Gaudier-Brzeska. The young Frenchman, who had added the name of his Polish mistress to the Gaudier to which he was born and who had spent the three years of his working career in England, was killed in battle on the Western Front while fighting with the French forces. Pound went on to the production of the voluminous writings that have been variously praised and denounced. The first of the epic *Cantos* was begun three years after Gaudier-Brzeska drew and sculpted his likeness.

Lent by Mr. Benjamin Sonnenberg, Jr.

RAPHAEL SOYER

TOMBOV, RUSSIA 1899 -

58 SELF-PORTRAIT WITH THE ARTIST'S FATHER

Pencil. 9¾ x 12⅛ inches.
Signed in pencil at lower right: *Raphael Soyer.*

Soyer's subject matter has always been the familiar: himself, his family, neighbors, and the city around him. The Sonnenberg drawing in expression, pose, and style recalls many of the self-portraits of the prints (see, for example, nos. 8, 73, and 116 in *Raphael Soyer: Fifty Years of Printmaking, 1917–1967*, edited by Sylvan Cole, Jr., New York, 1967), but no specifically related lithograph or etching was made. The man to the artist's left, who so closely resembles him, is his father, a Hebrew teacher and writer who taught both of his sons, Raphael and Moses, to draw before they came to the United States in 1916. Often portrayed by his son, he is a shadowy rather than a real presence here, and recent conversation with the artist confirms that he died some years before this touching "Double Portrait" – to use the artist's title – was made.

Exhibitions: New York, Babcock Galleries, "Raphael Soyer: Retrospective Exhibition, 1926–1956," 1956, no. 53, repr. on cover.

FELIKS TOPOLSKI

CZESTOCHOWA 1907 -

59 E. M. FORSTER AND BENJAMIN BRITTEN 1879-1970. 1913-

Pen and brown ink. 9¾ x 7¾ inches (sight).
Signed in gray ink at lower right: *Feliks Topolski.* Inscribed in pencil at upper right, *E. M. Forster*; at lower left, *Benjamin Britten.*

The Polish-born draughtsman, who has lived in London since 1935, has depicted hundreds of twentieth-century happenings and personalities in a kind of virtuoso pictorial journalism. His double portrait of E. M. Forster and Benjamin Britten stresses a resemblance which in actuality was more intellectual than physical. Just as music was the writer-novelist's favorite art, so Britten has always worked closely with men of letters. His working relationship with W. H. Auden began in the thirties when he wrote incidental music for Auden's movie scripts and plays and also for Louis MacNeice, Edward Sackville-West, and Christopher Isherwood. Since then poetry, including Auden's and Donne's, has provided both inspiration and lyrics for his own work. Forster, who wrote about the composer's opera, *Peter Grimes*, collaborated with Eric Crozier on the libretto of another of Britten's operas, *Billy Budd* (Covent Garden, 1951). The author of *A Passage to India* died June 7, 1970.

60 DAME EDITH AND SIR OSBERT SITWELL 1887-1964. 1892-1969

Pen and faded gray-blue ink. 6¾ x 5⅝ inches.
Signed and dated in pencil at lower right: *Feliks Topolski / 47.*

Topolski's rapid notation of the Sitwell profiles brings to mind a pointed remark likening them to a pair of extinct birds. Born into an aristocratic family, Dame Edith and her brothers, Osbert and Sacheverell, set out early to distinguish themselves and to revitalize the world of letters — this aim was shared by their *habitués*, Ezra Pound, T. S. Eliot, and Wyndham Lewis. Dame Edith frequently appeared in costumes of medieval inspiration to accentuate what she described as her "Plantagenet features." The Sitwells and their accomplishments are well-known from the writings of both brother and sister, most memorably perhaps from Sir Osbert's five autobiographical works. All three Sitwells wrote poetry — from 1916 on, Dame Edith edited *Wheels*, an annual anthology, chiefly a vehicle for her own verse and that of her brothers.

61 JACOB EPSTEIN. 1880-1959

Charcoal. 19 x 12½ inches.

Signed at lower right: *Feliks Topolski.* Inscribed at upper right: *Jacob Epstein.*

The loose calligraphy of this portrait is peculiarly expressive in its suggestion of the sagging features of the aged sculptor, seen in younger guise in no. 41.

SAUL STEINBERG

RAMNIC-SARAT, RUMANIA 1914 -

62 BENJAMIN SONNENBERG. 1901-

Pen and black ink on white paper. 13 x 10 inches.

Signed in pen and ink at lower right: *Steinberg.*

Steinberg made this drawing to accompany Geoffrey T. Hellman's profile of Mr. Sonnenberg entitled "A House on Gramercy Park," which appeared in *The New Yorker* of April 8, 1950. There the collector is described as "a short, rotund man," who dresses "counter to the trend" and who "has increased the individuality of his appearance by cultivating a walrus mustache," all good copy for the caricaturist's nimble pen as Steinberg effectively demonstrated. The Rumanian-born draughtsman, a graduate in architecture from the University of Milan, 1940, has been on the staff of *The New Yorker* since 1941, producing sometimes as many as thirty drawings a year for its pages, and working as well for other publications.

Mr. Sonnenberg has been drawn in more conventional vein by Eric (C. O. A. Erickson), and Leonard Baskin once penned a likeness of him in the margin of a letter.

Exhibitions: Poughkeepsie, New York, Vassar College, "Drawings and Watercolors from Alumnae and Their Families," 1961, no. 154, repr.

Lent by Mr. Benjamin Sonnenberg, Jr.

MICHAEL AYRTON

LONDON 1921 -

63 WYNDHAM LEWIS. 1884-1957

Pencil. 9½ x 13½ inches.

Signed and dated in pencil at lower left: *michael ayrton / 1955.*

Wyndham Lewis had a double career — as an artist working in a semi-abstract style and as a satirical novelist, essayist, and vitriolic critic. He was constantly engaged in controversy, in politics as well as in matters of artistic and literary import. Attracted to certain aspects of Hitlerism, as Pound had been to Mussolini, he was once termed "that lonely old volcano of the Right" by W. H. Auden. His life as an artist was crowned in 1956 by a large retrospective exhibition "Wyndham Lewis and Vorticism" at the Tate Gallery. "Old Vort," as Ezra Pound (see no. 57) addressed him from the latter's "Washington prison," was at this time in ill-health and blind, and so he is seen in this portrait by a young friend and artistic ally. There is no trace of the "lean Spanish elegance" which Sir Osbert Sitwell (see no. 60) ascribed to him as a young man, nor much of his later "robust and rather jocose Dutch convexity," but something of his lively pugnacity still makes itself felt despite the encumbrance of the heavy glasses and eyeshade.

Ayrton, an artist now working principally as a sculptor, first met Lewis in 1946, after the appearance of his book *British Drawings* where Lewis's draughtsmanship was lauded. Over the next decade, the two artists traded favorable reviews and notices of each other's work, and Lewis commissioned Ayrton to design the jackets for his last books and to illustrate *The Human Age*. A drawing made at the same time as this one is reproduced on the title page of Geoffrey Wagner, *A Portrait of the Artist as Enemy*, New Haven, 1957. Ayrton also painted the blind Lewis.

64 DYLAN THOMAS. 1914-1953

Pencil. 11 x 6½ inches.

Signed and inscribed in pencil by the artist across lower edge: *For Hilda / with love — in memory of Dylan / Michael Ayrton.*

What Ayrton saw in the gifted, roisterous Welsh poet seems to have been "the complete bohemian, scorning the accustomed virtues of respectability: and carrying his insignia of defiance unashamedly and sometimes provocatively — his seaman's jersey — his old tweed coat — his flannels — his cigarette and his pint" [part of a description by A. G. Prys-Jones, published *Dock Leaves* (Pembroke), Spring, 1954]. Poet and artist do not appear to have been in strong rapport, at least on occasion, if one is to judge from Ayrton's report that "in a public house . . . Dylan Thomas . . . almost tearfully requested me *not* to make a drawing to accompany a poem of his in a magazine" (*Golden Sections*, London, 1957, p. 144).

The portrait is inscribed to Mr. Sonnenberg's wife.

INDEX OF ARTISTS

Ayrton, Michael 63, 64
Beerbohm, Sir Max 39
Biddle, George 54, 55
Boldini, Giovanni 22, 23, 24
Brangwyn, Sir Frank 36
Burne-Jones, Sir Edward 13, 14
Cassatt, Mary 21
Cézanne, Paul 17, 18
Chassériau, Théodore 7
Courbet, Gustave 6
David, Jacques-Louis 1
Degas, Edgar 16
Delacroix, Eugène 5
Dodd, Francis 40, 41
Doré, Gustave 12
Dufy, Raoul 45
Feuerbach, Anselm 10
Gaudier-Brzeska, Henri 57
Gauguin, Paul 26
Gogh, Vincent van 27
Greaves, Walter 25
Hartley, Marsden 44
Ingres, Jean-Auguste-Dominique 4
John, Sir Augustus 46, 47, 48
John, Gwen 42
La Fresnaye, Roger de 56
Lawrence, Sir Thomas 3
Lewis, Wyndham 52, 53
Luce, Maximilien 30, 31
Millais, Sir John Everett 9
Modigliani, Amedeo 50, 51
Morisot, Berthe 20
Pissarro, Camille 11
Prud'hon, Pierre-Paul 2
Robinson, Boardman 43
Rossetti, Dante Gabriel 8
Sargent, John Singer 28, 29
Seurat, Georges-Pierre 33
Sickert, Walter Richard 34
Signac, Paul 35
Solomon, Simeon 19
Soyer, Raphael 58
Steinberg, Saul 62
Steinlen, Théophile-Alexandre 32
Stella, Joseph 49
Topolski, Feliks 59, 60, 61
Vuillard, Edouard 37, 38
Whistler, James Abbott McNeill 15

INDEX OF SUBJECTS

Appert, Mme 33
Barrymore, Ethel 29
Basler, Adolphe 45
Beerbohm, Sir Max 34
Bibesco, Princess Marthe 37
Biddle, George 43
Biron, Le Marquis de 24
Blanche, Jacques-Emile 22
Brangwyn, Sir Frank 36
Britten, Benjamin 59
Campbell, Roy 52
Carlyle, Thomas 25
Cézanne, Mme 17
Cézanne, Paul 18
Chocquet, Victor 17
Conrad, Joseph 39
Cross, Henry E. 31
Debussy, Claude 32
Degas, Edgar 23
Degas, Marguerite 16
Epstein, Sir Jacob 41, 61
Forster, E. M. 59
George IV 3
Hartley, Marsden 44
John, Sir Augustus 46

Kohler, M. 50
La Fresnaye, Roger de 56
Lee, Vernon 21
Lewis, Mrs. Wyndham 53
Lewis, Wyndham 63
Luce, Maximilien 35
Marcotte de Quivières, Louis 7
Morrell, Lady Ottoline 47
Natanson, Thadée 38
Origo, Marchesa Iris 48
Polidori, Eliza Harriet 8
Pope Pius VII 1
Pound, Ezra 57
Ramel, M. and Mme Edme 4
Saint-Gaudens, Augustus 28
Santayana, George 54
Seurat, Mme 33
Signac, Paul 30
Sitwell, Dame Edith 60
Sitwell, Sir Osbert 60
Sommariva, Count 2
Sonnenberg, Benjamin 62
Soyer, Raphael 58
Symons, Arthur 42
Thomas, Dylan 64
Whistler, James Abbott McNeill 15
Wilson, Edmund 55
Woolf, Virginia 40

PLATES

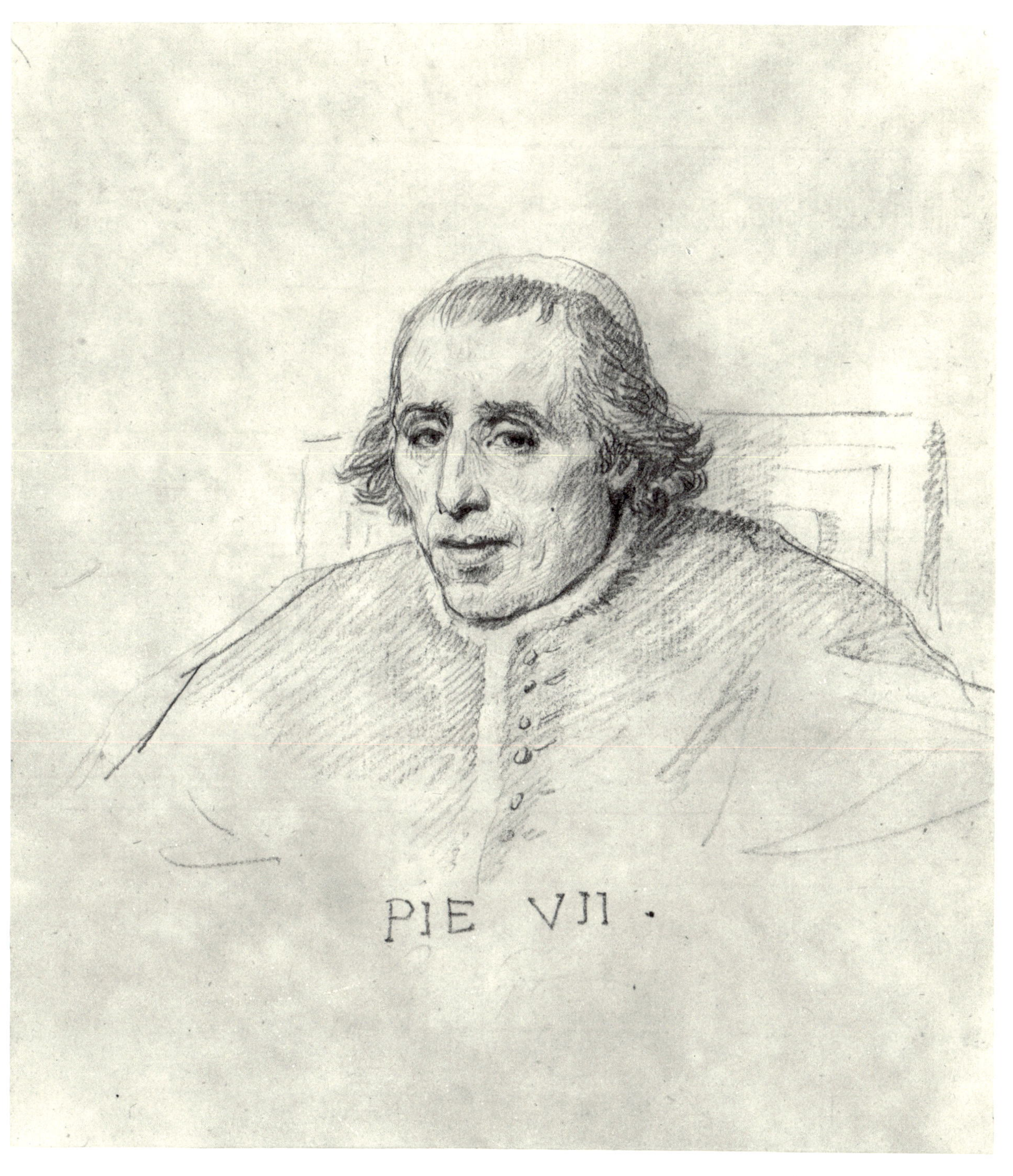

1 Jacques-Louis David. *Pope Pius VII*

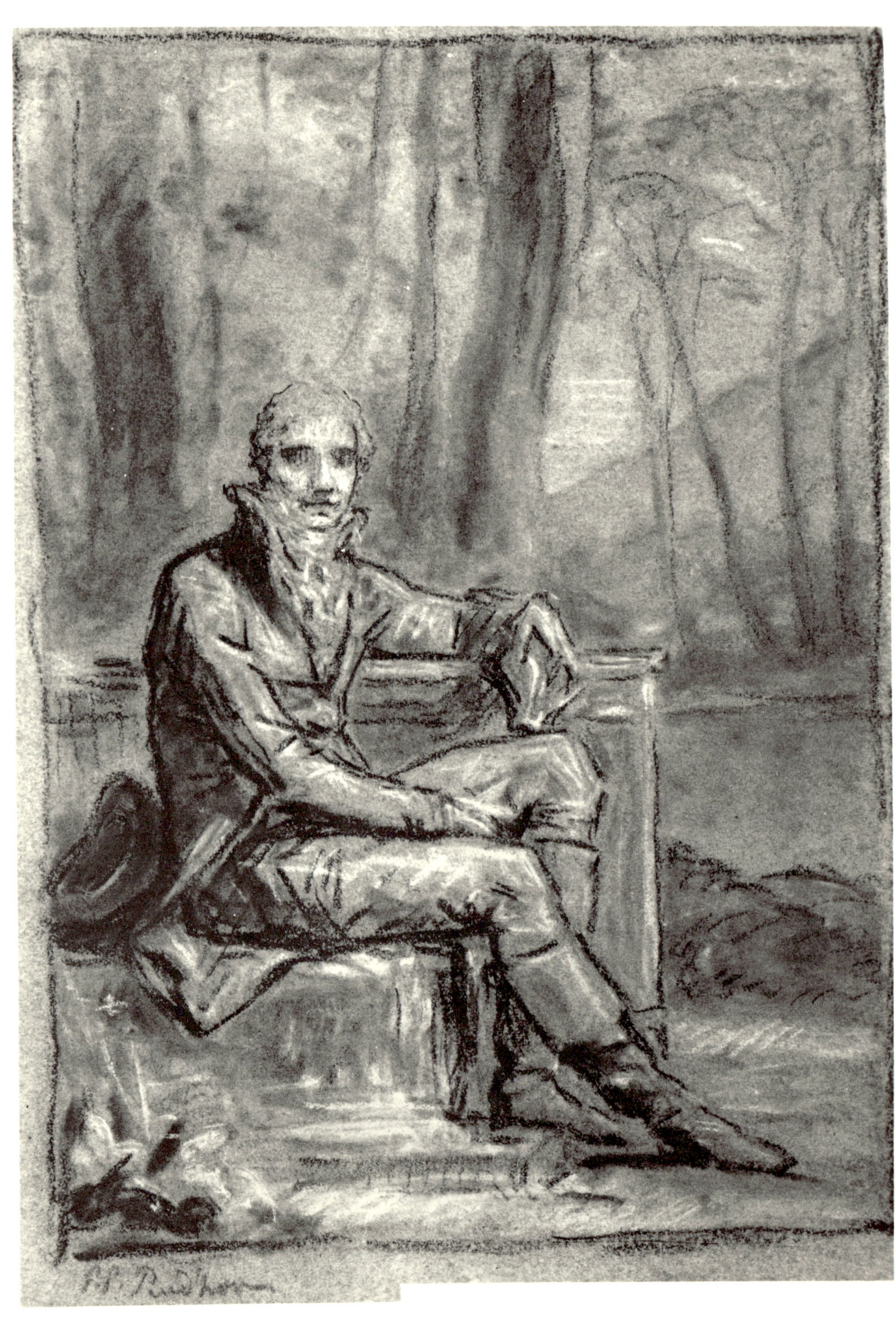

2 Pierre-Paul Prud'hon. *Count Sommariva*

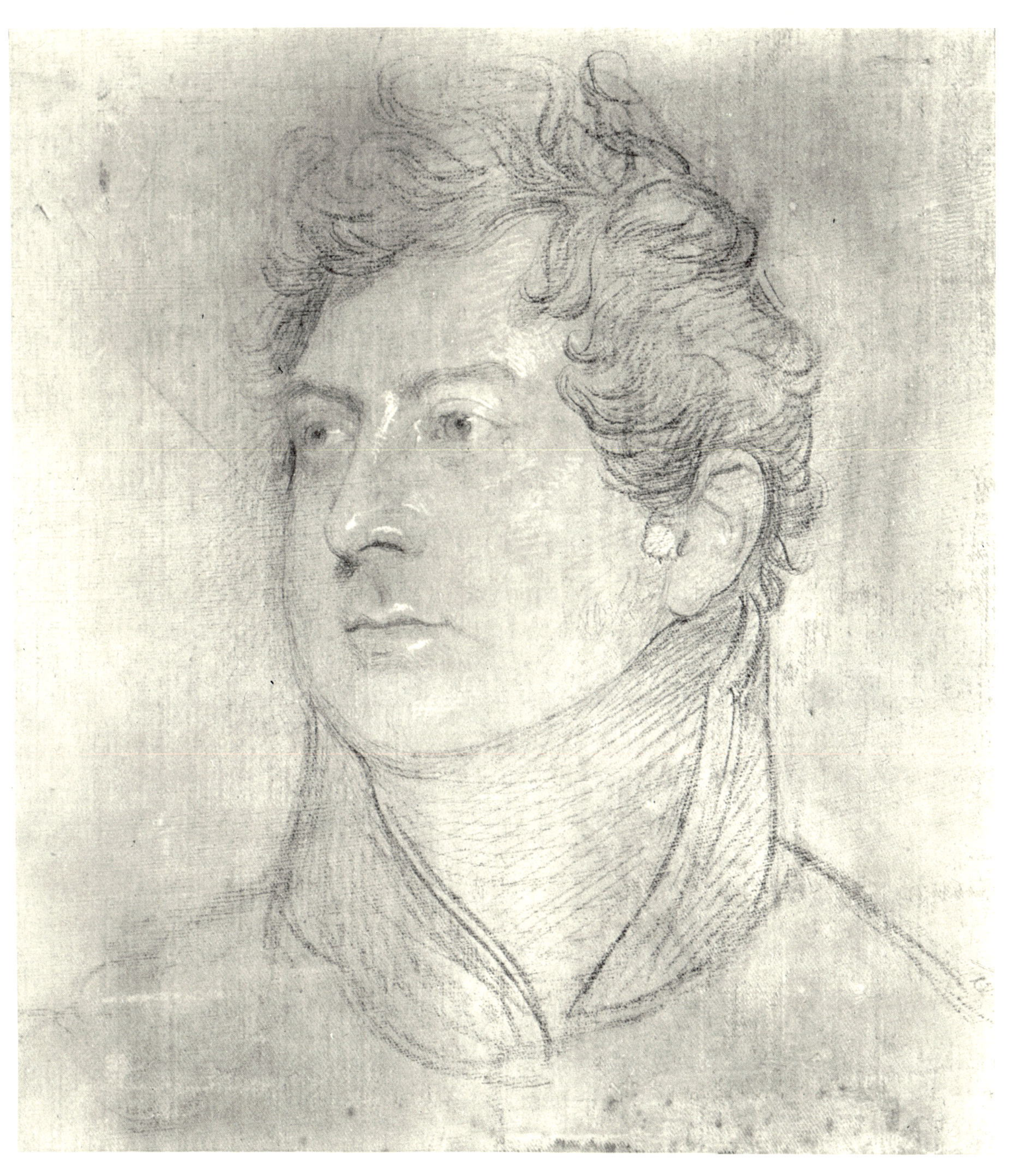

3 Sir Thomas Lawrence. *George IV*

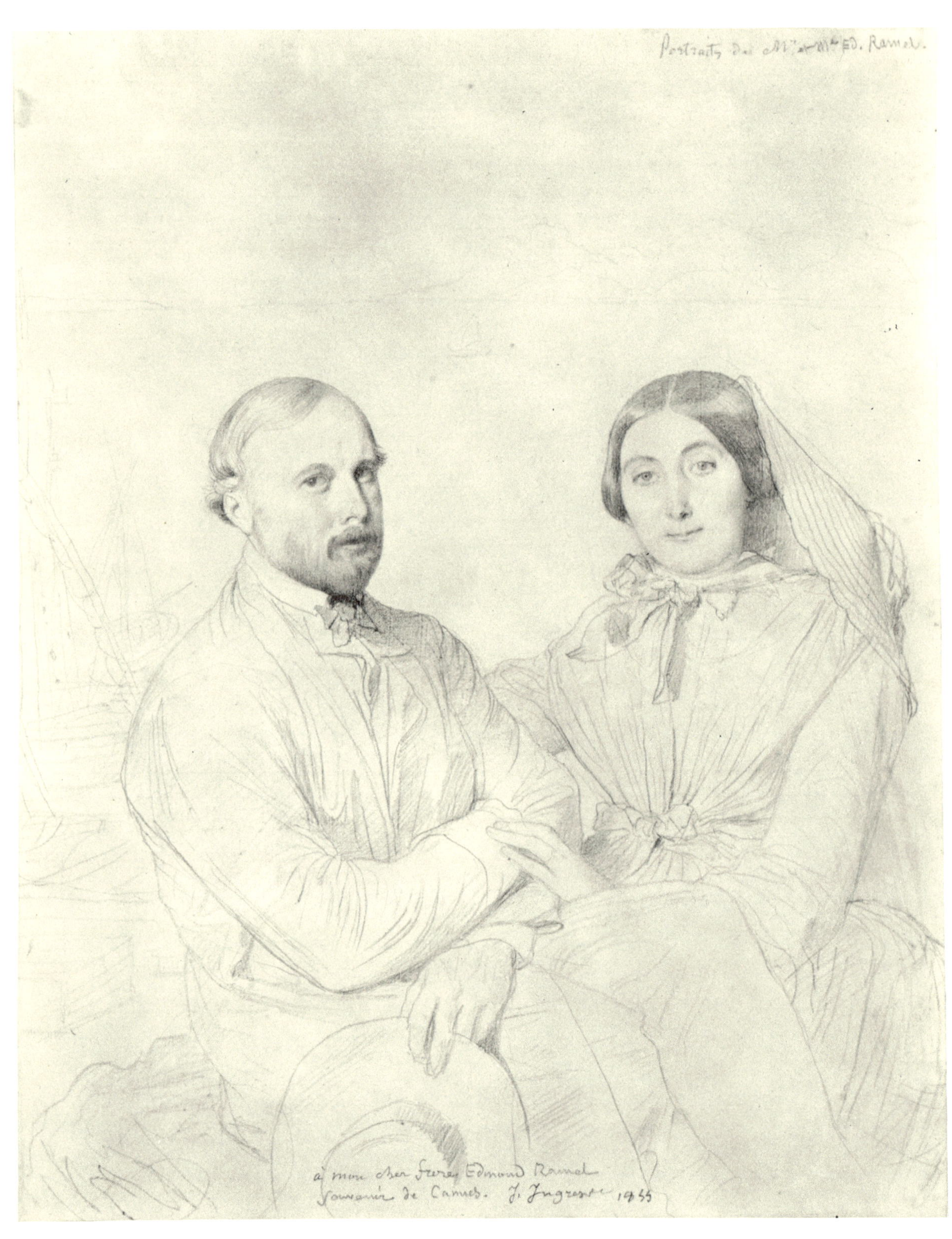

4 Jean-Auguste-Dominique Ingres. *M. and Mme Edme Ramel*

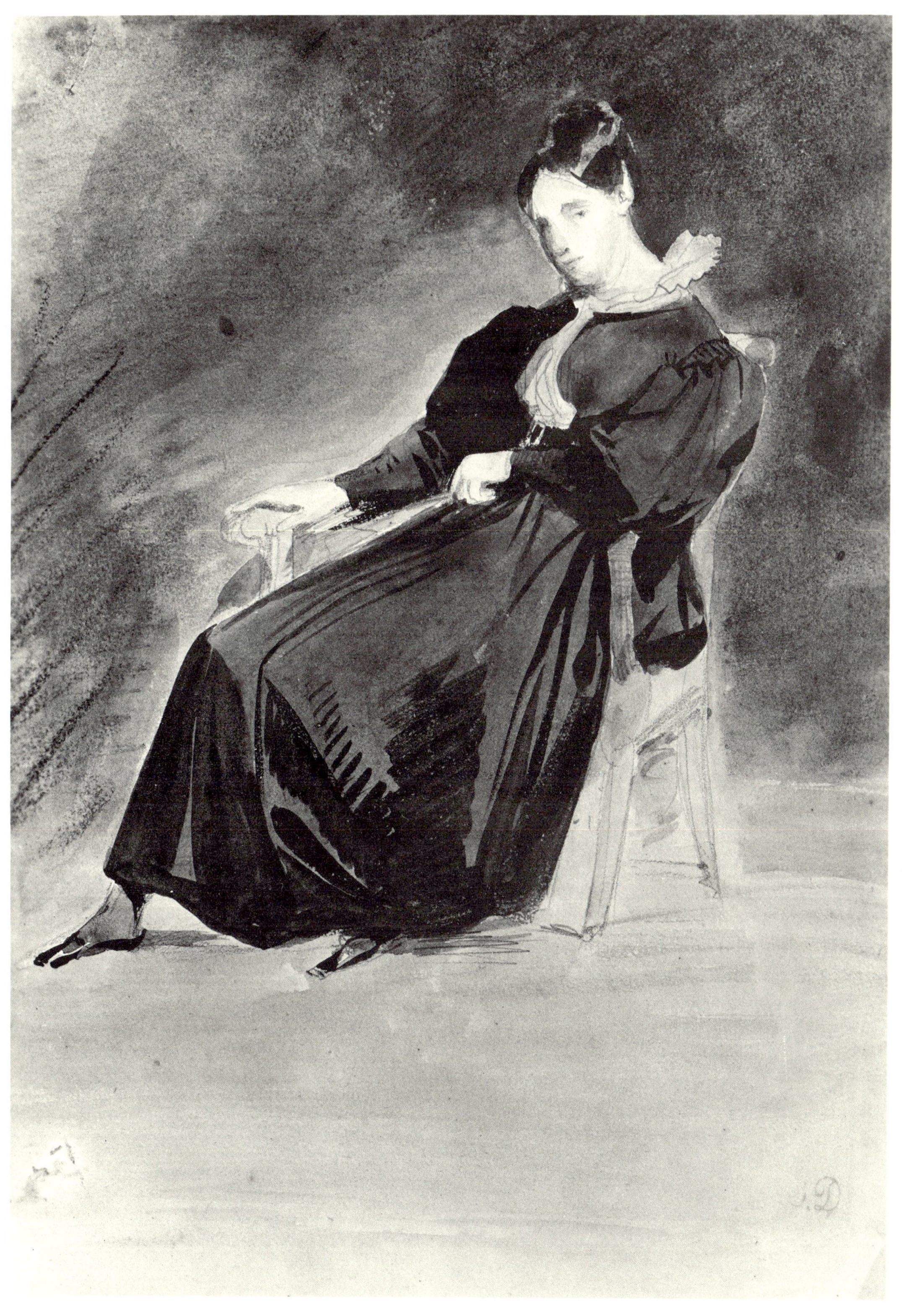

5 Eugène Delacroix. *Seated Young Woman*

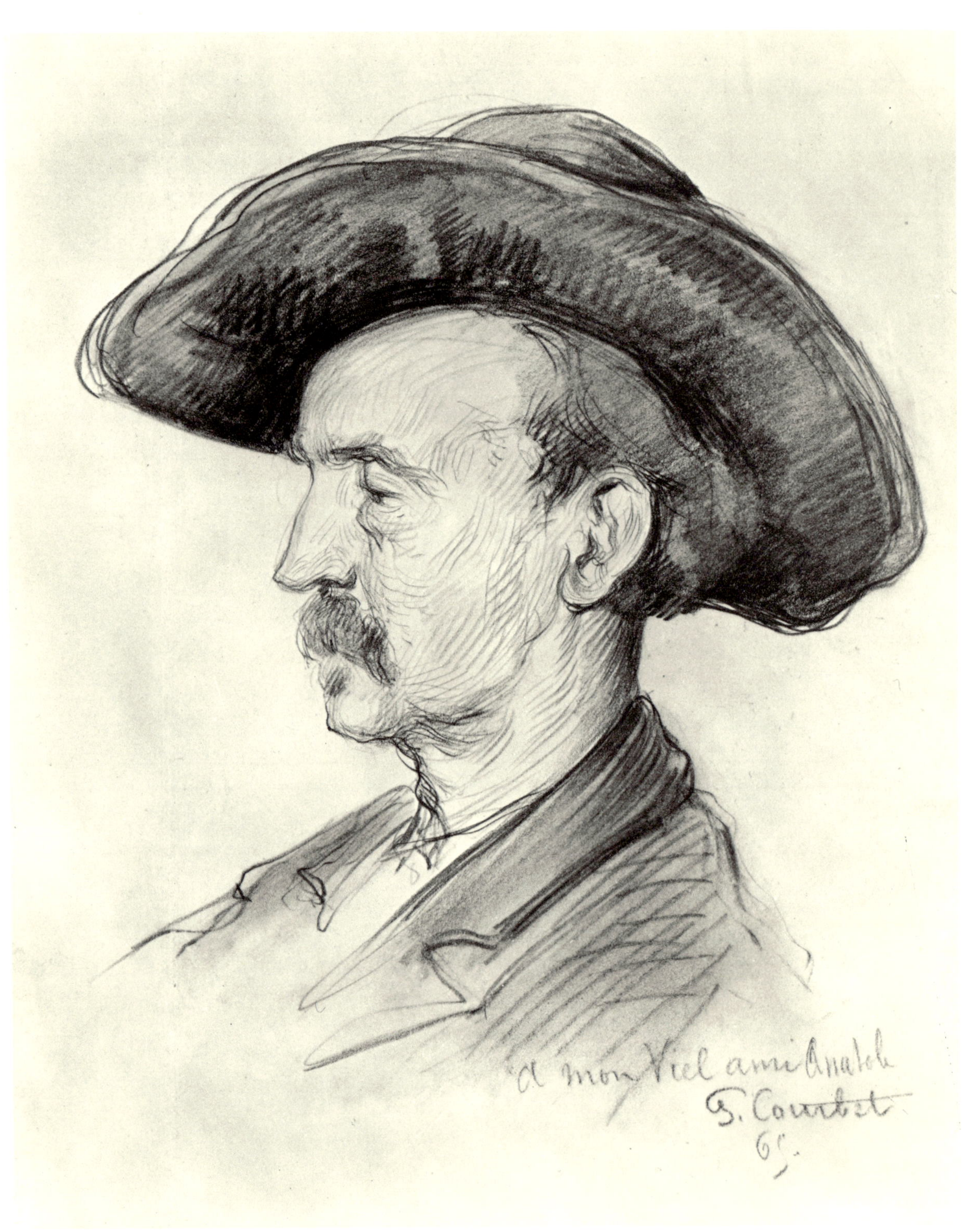

6 Gustave Courbet. "*Anatole*"

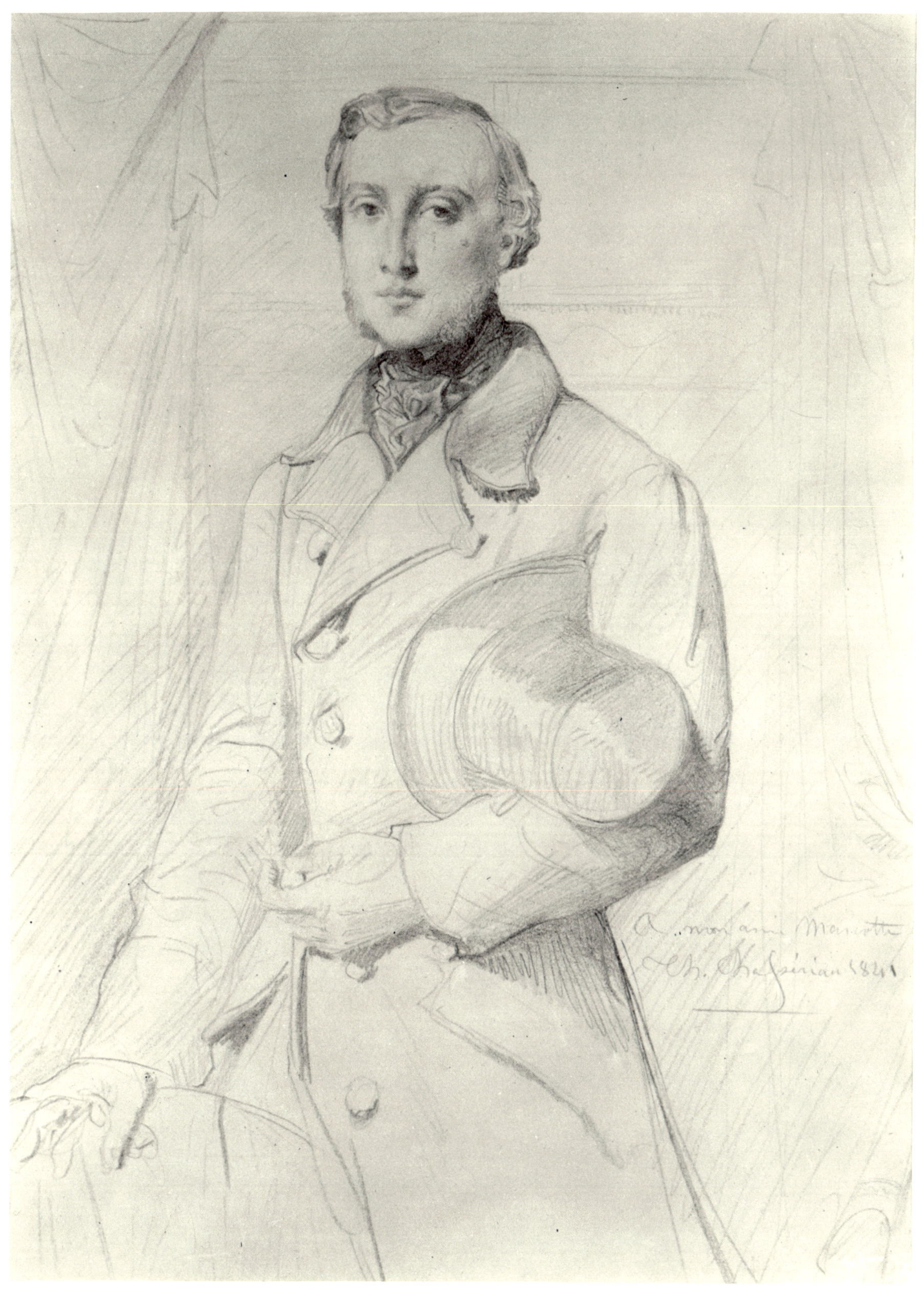

7 Théodore Chassériau. *Louis Marcotte de Quivières*

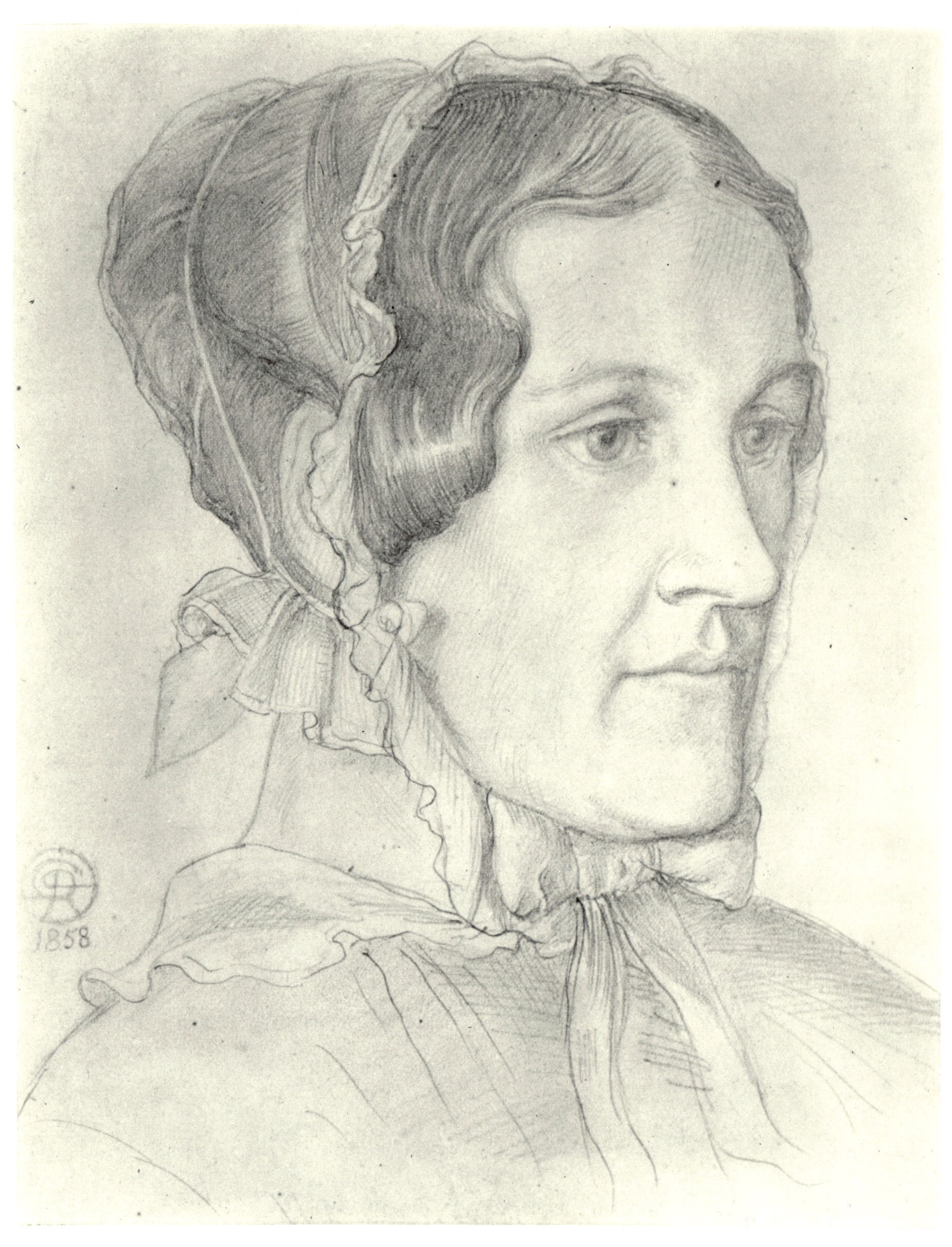

8 Dante Gabriel Rossetti. *Eliza Harriet Polidori, the Artist's Aunt*

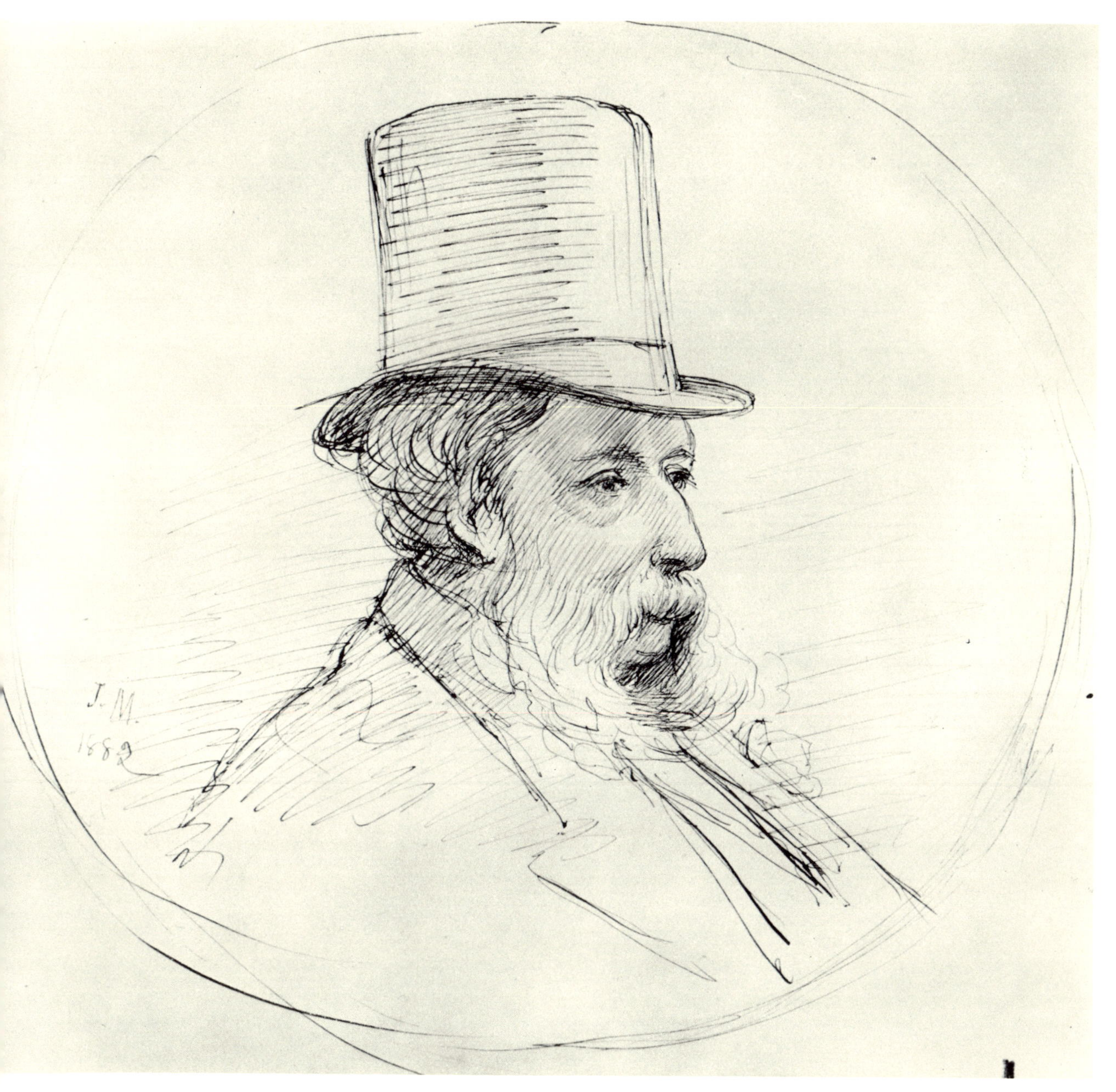

9 Sir John Everett Millais. *Man in a Top Hat*

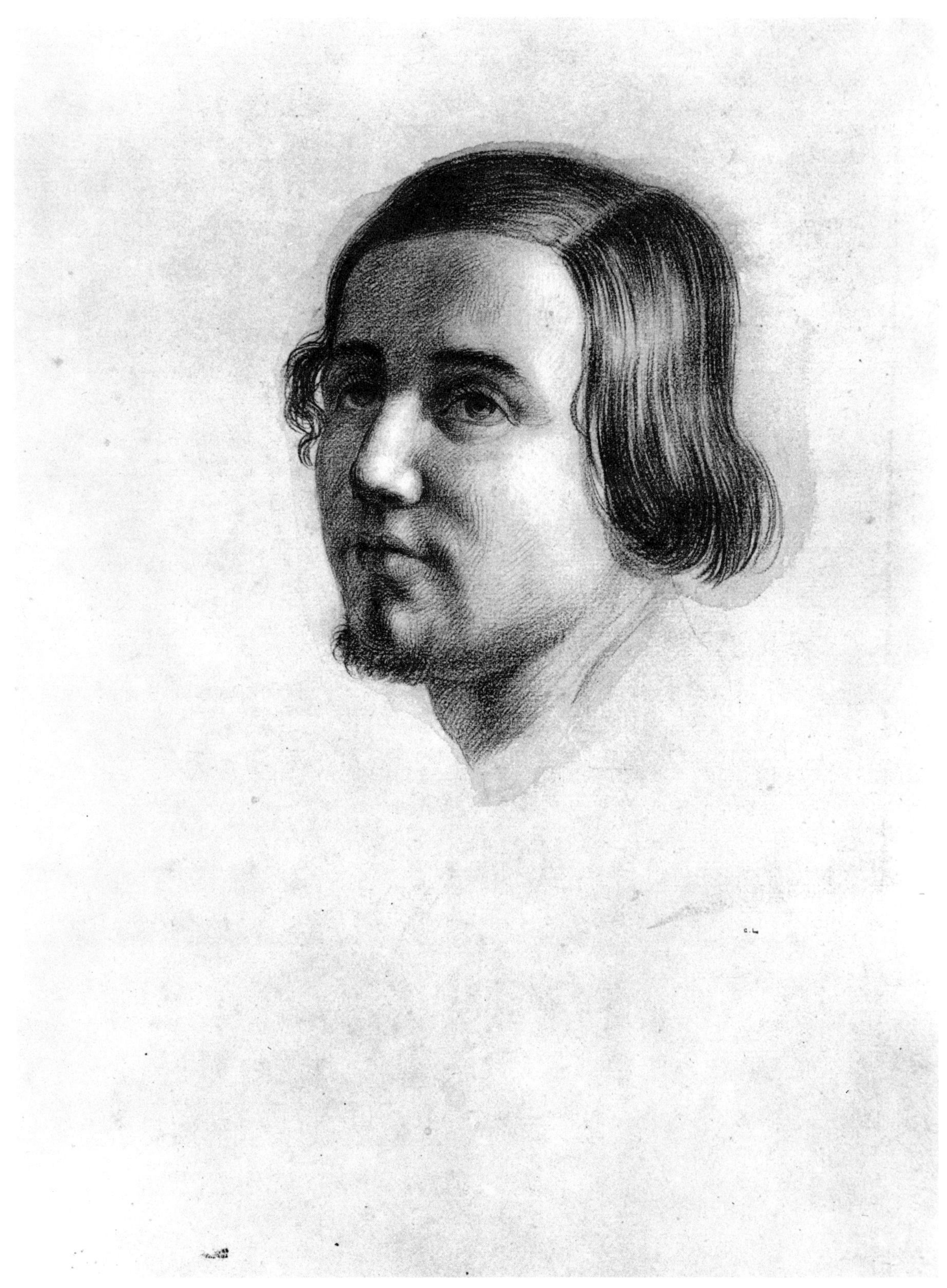

10 Anselm Feuerbach. *Head of a Man*

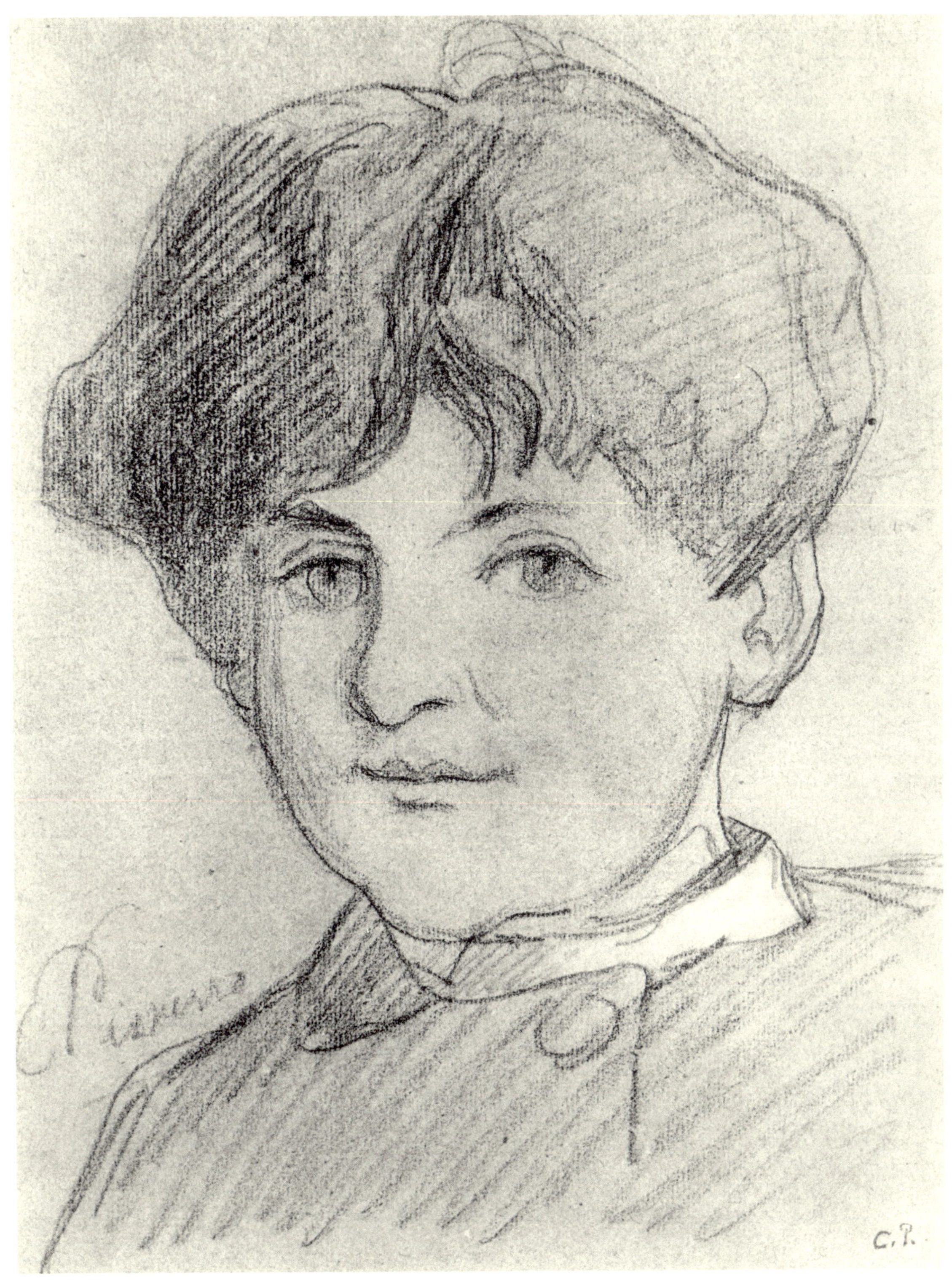

11 Camille Pissarro. *Head of a Boy*

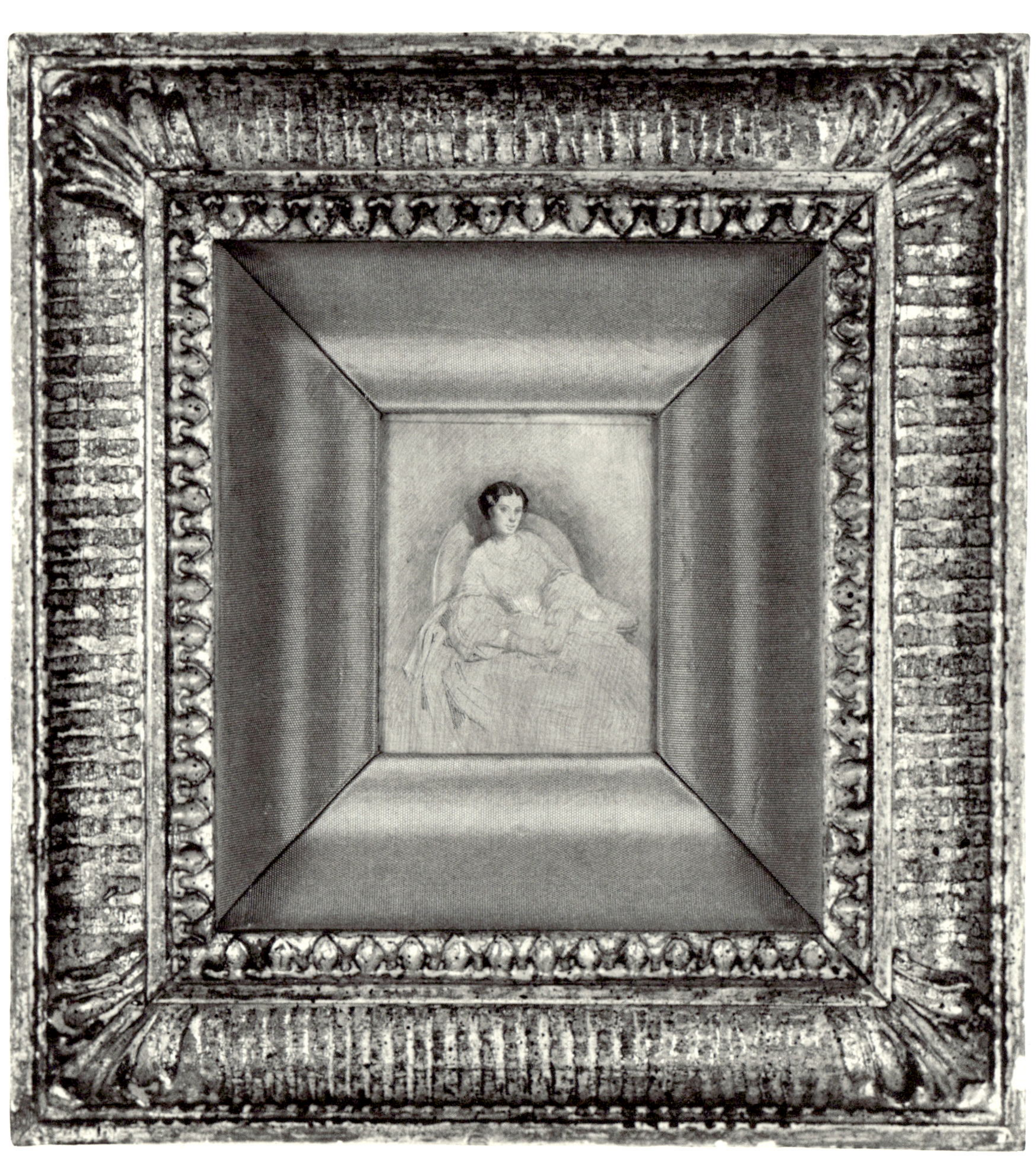

12 Gustave Doré. *Seated Lady*

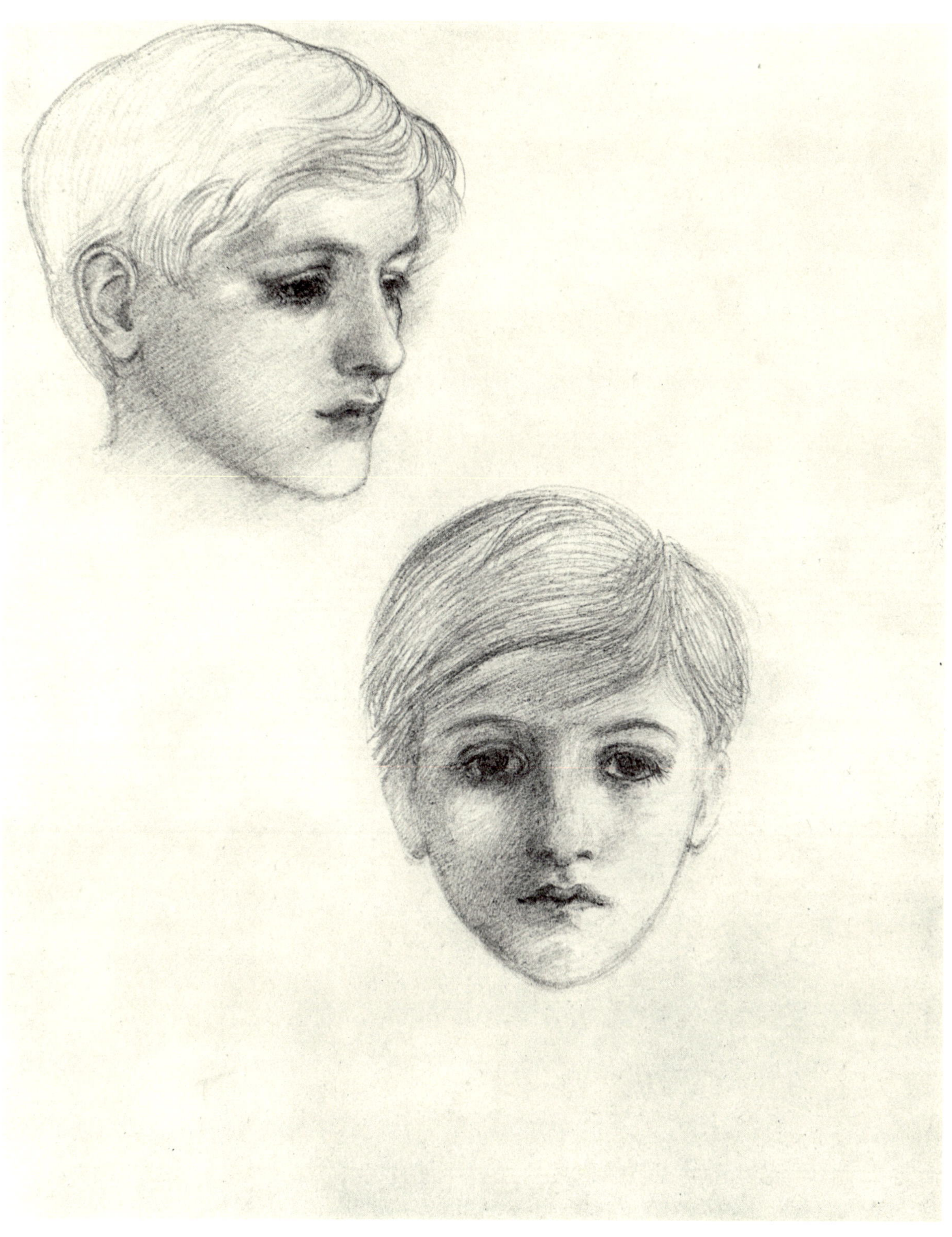

13 Sir Edward Burne-Jones. *Studies of a Boy's Head*

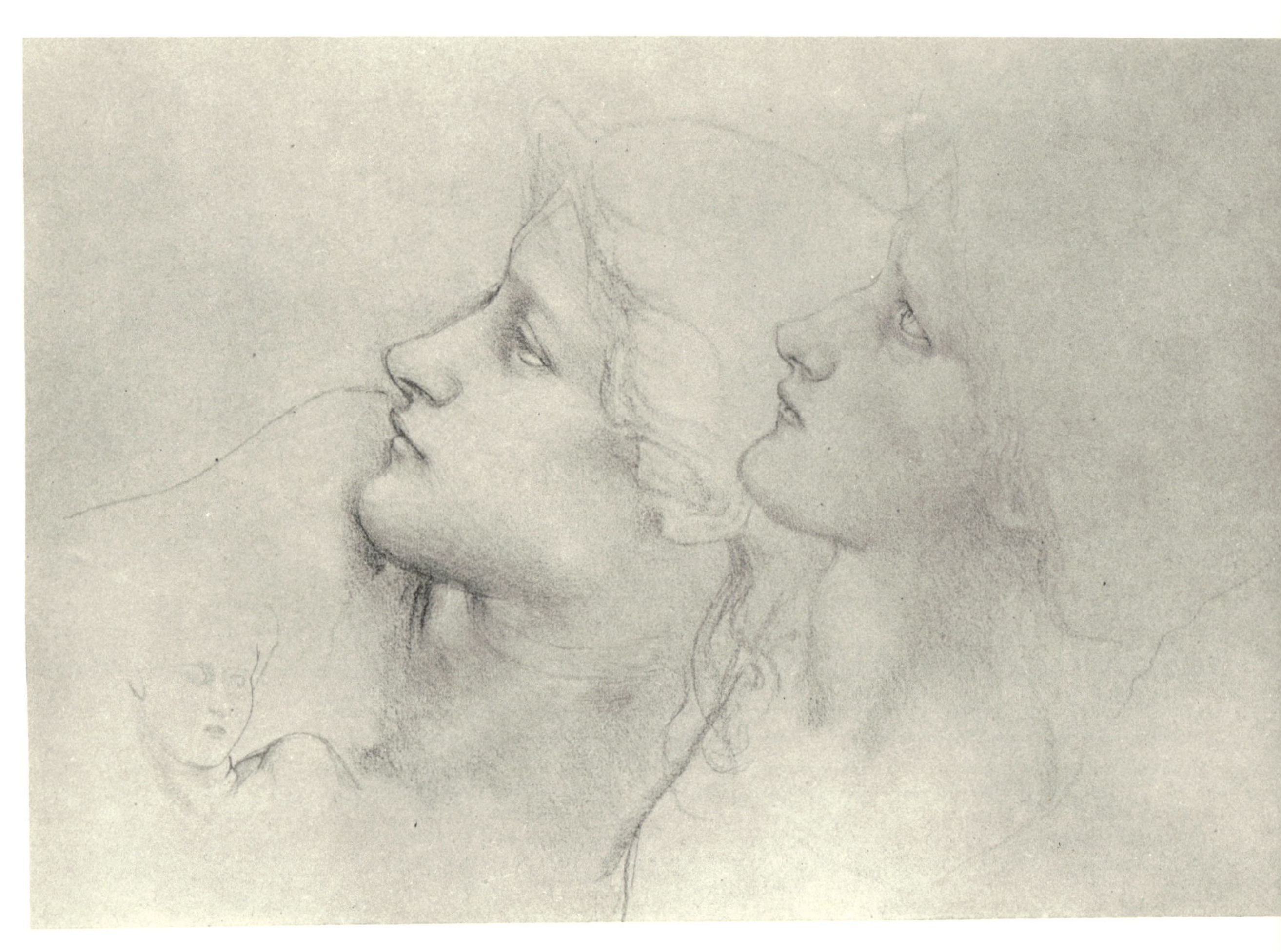

14 Sir Edward Burne-Jones. *Studies for* Andromeda

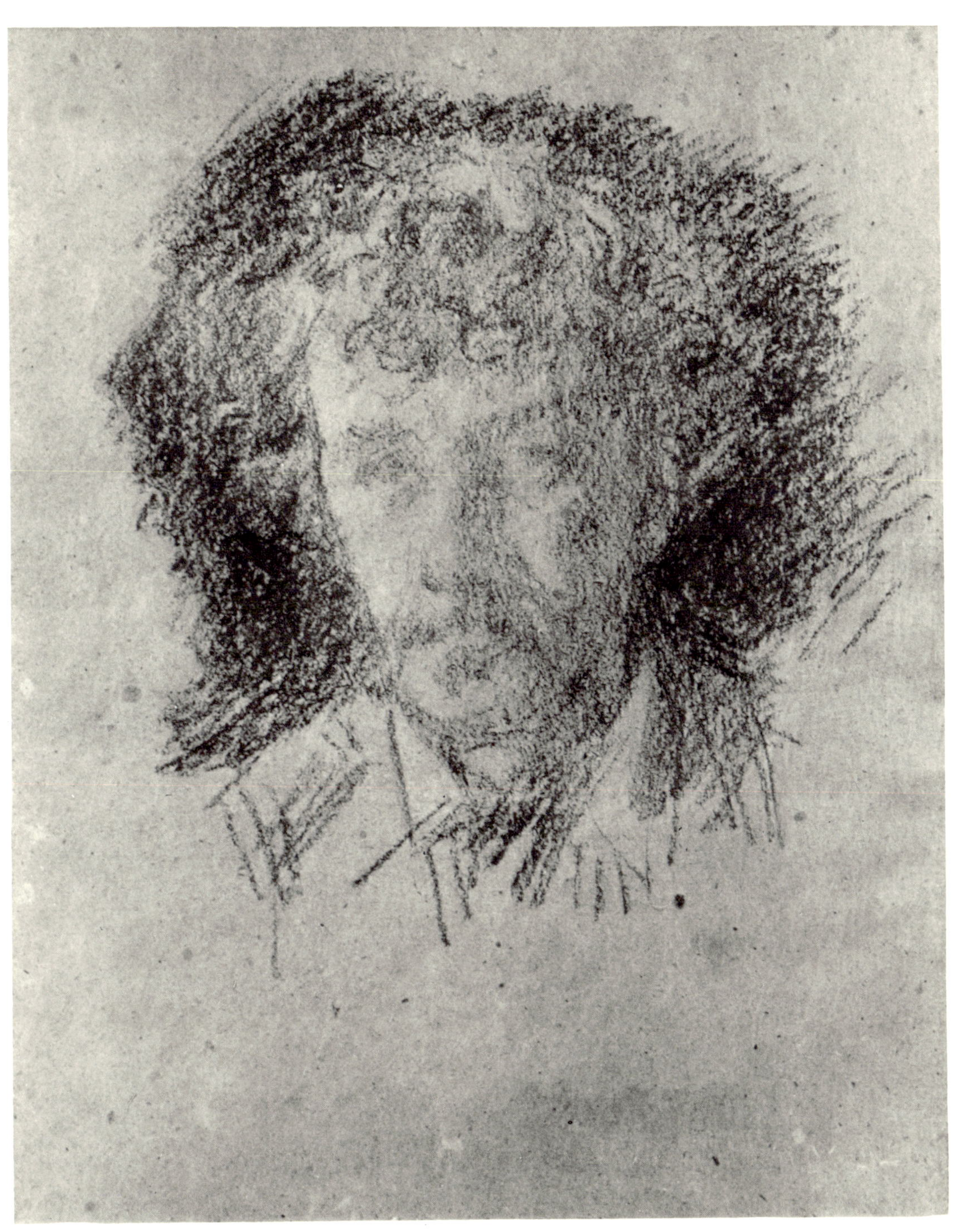

15 James Abbott McNeill Whistler. *Self-Portrait*

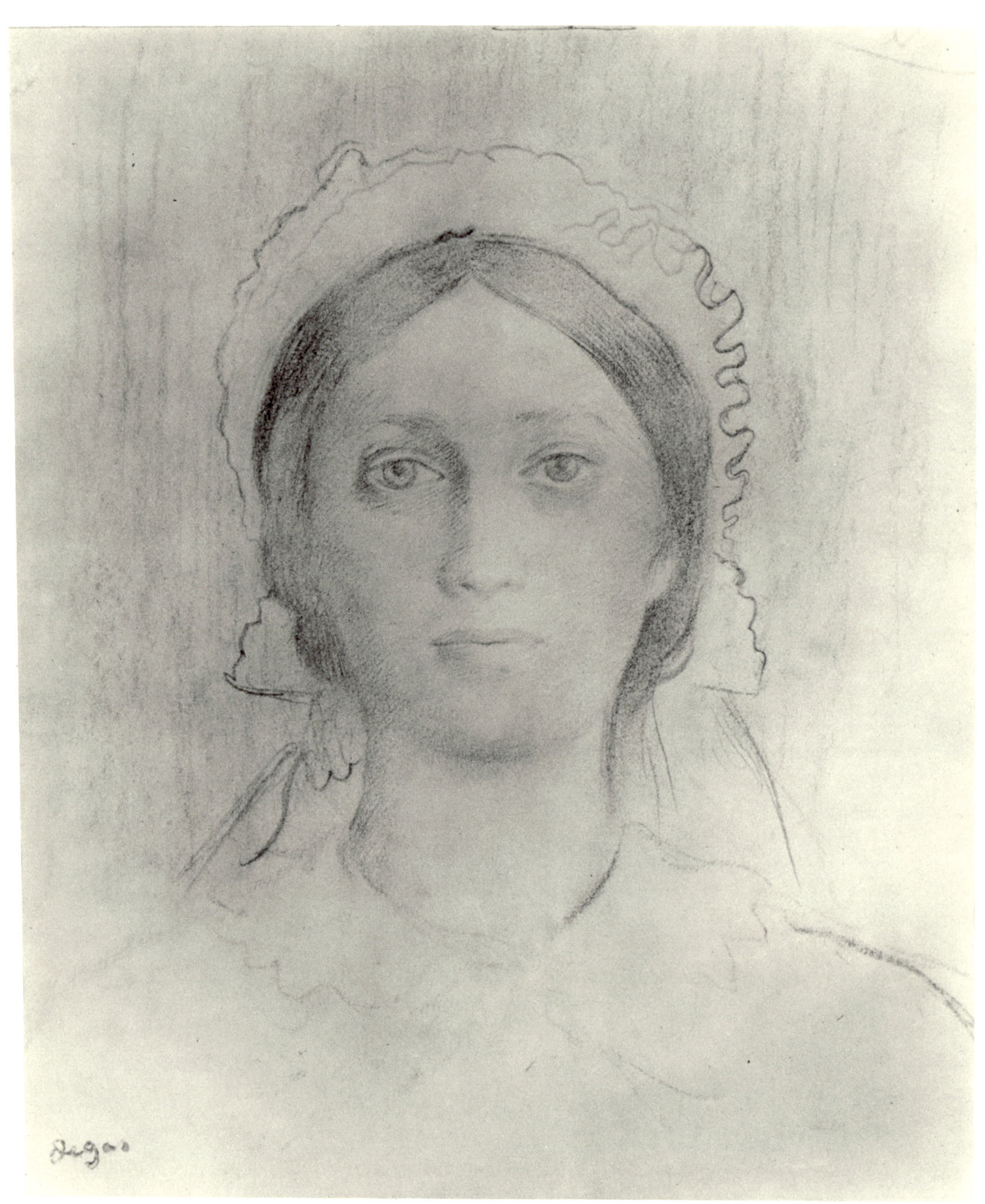

16 Edgar Degas. *Marguerite Degas, later Mme Henri Fevre*

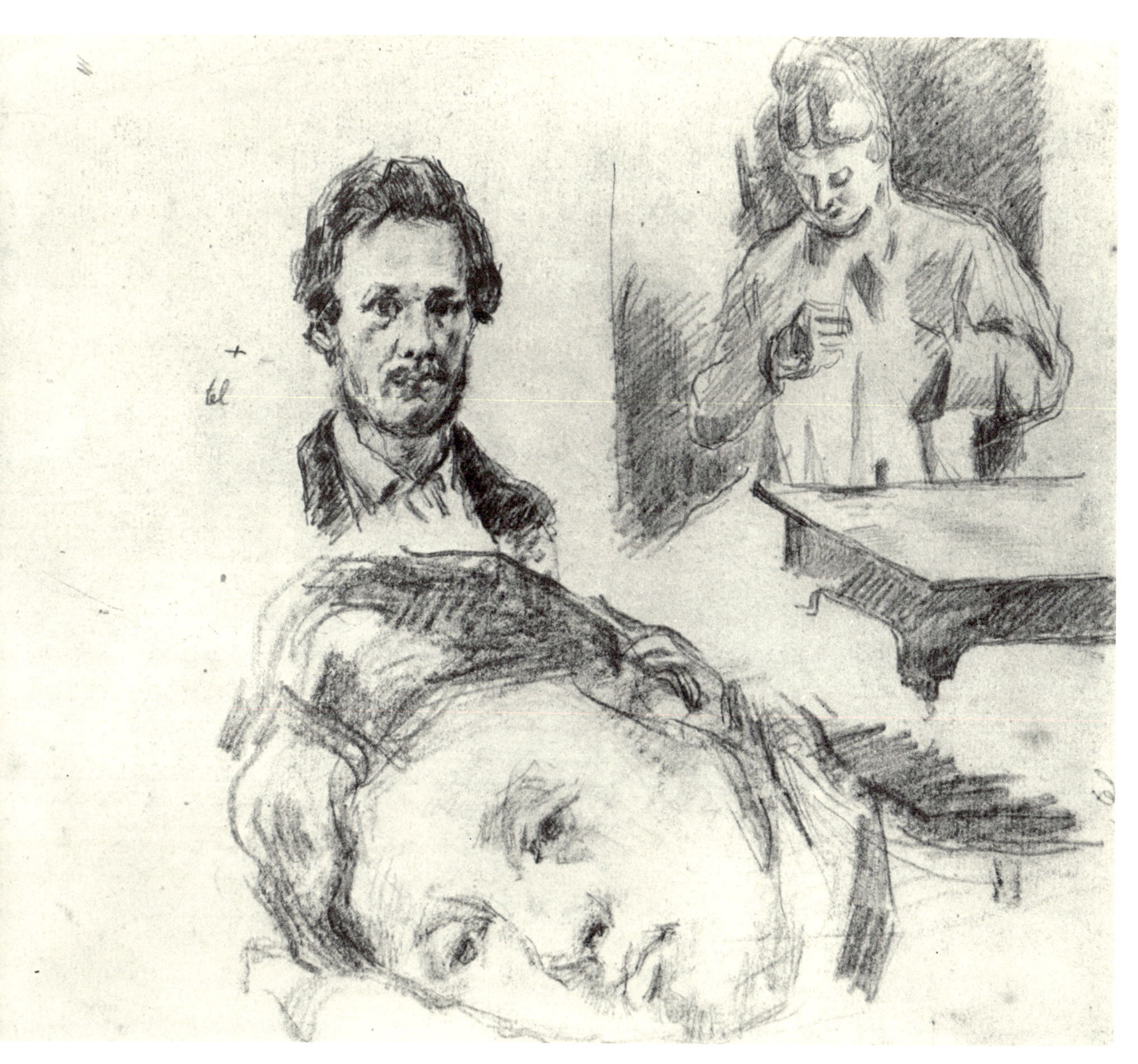

17 Paul Cézanne. *Two studies of Mme Cézanne, and M. Chocquet*

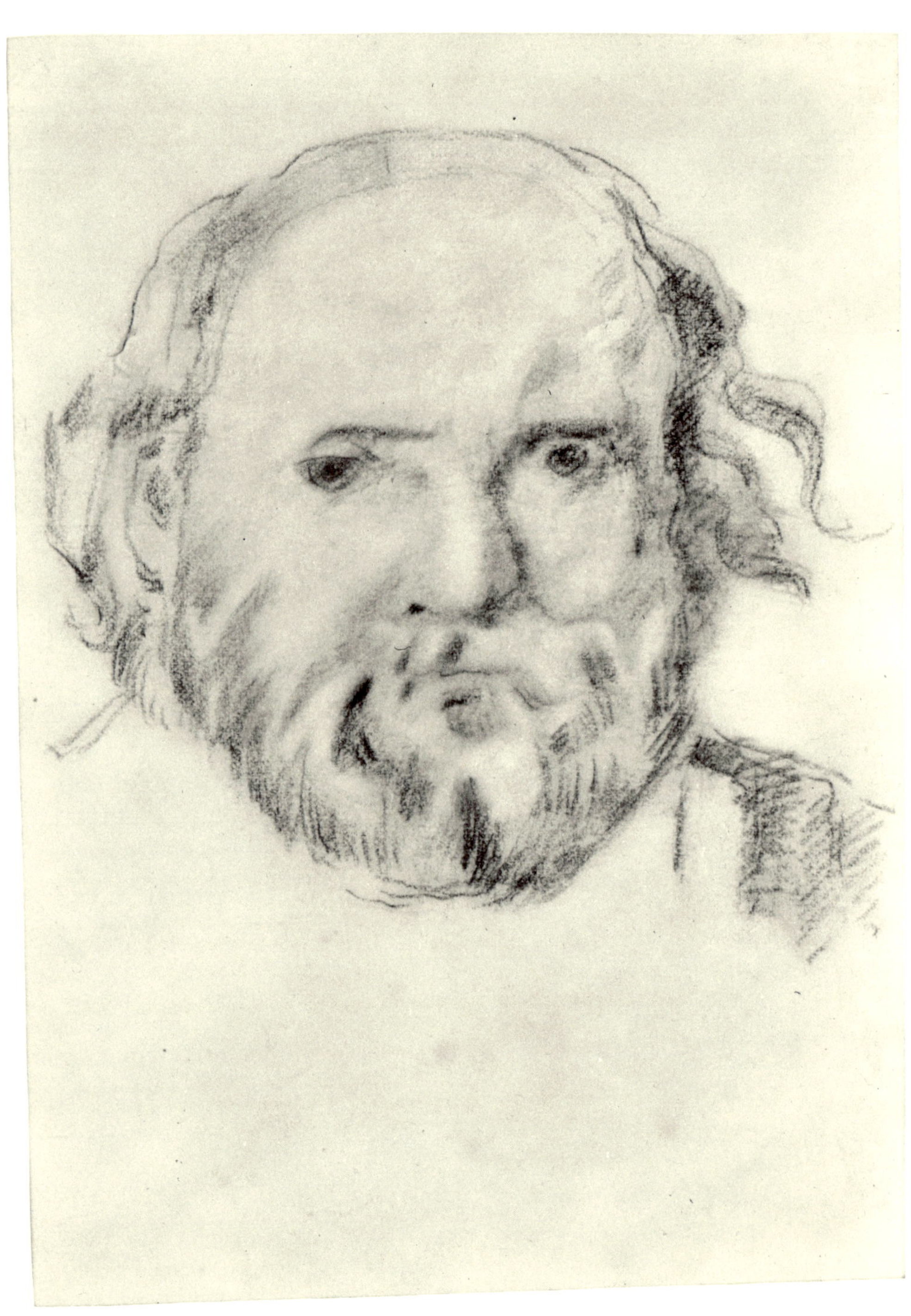

18 Paul Cézanne. *Self-Portrait*

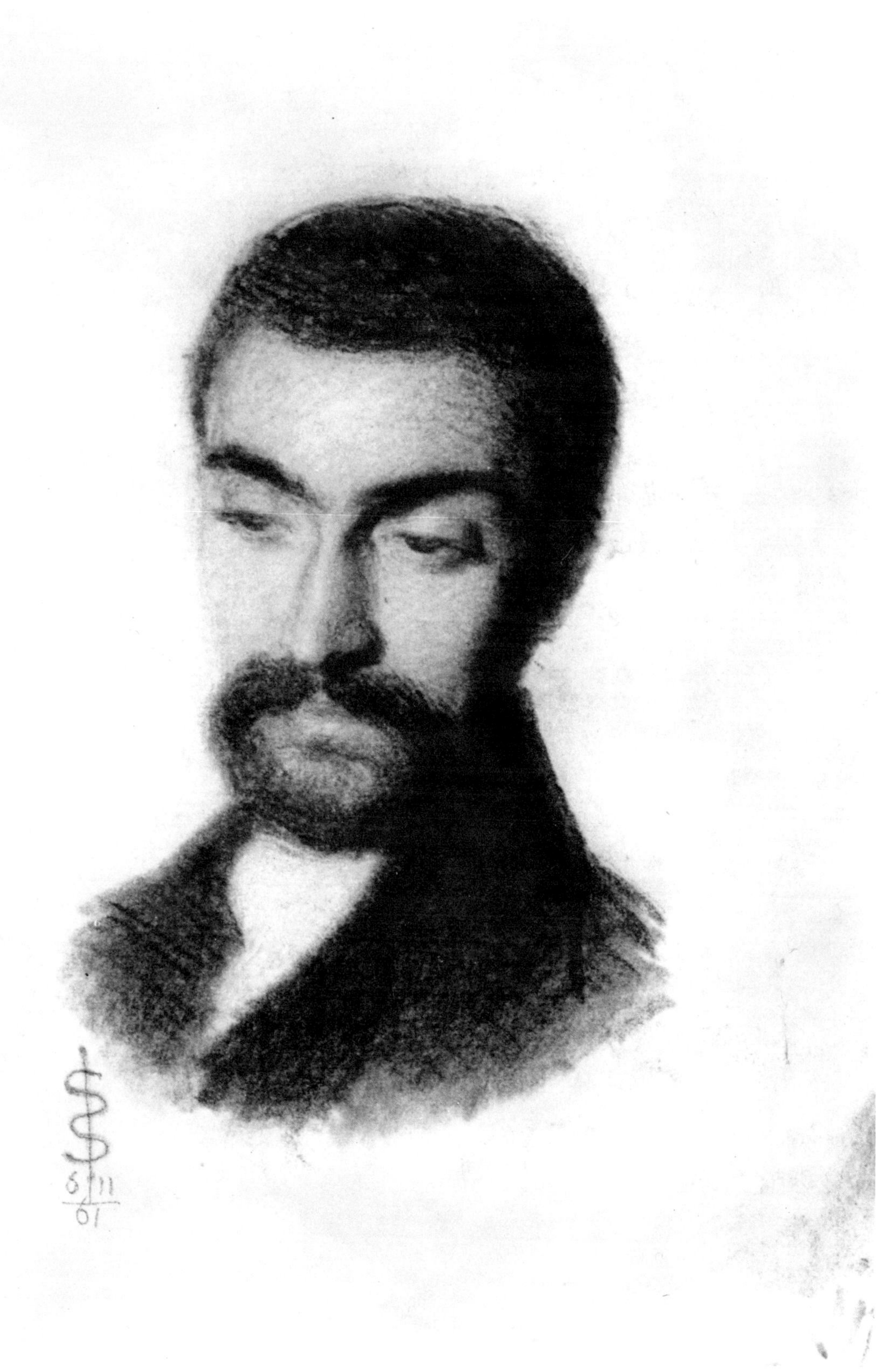

19 Simeon Solomon. *Bearded Man*

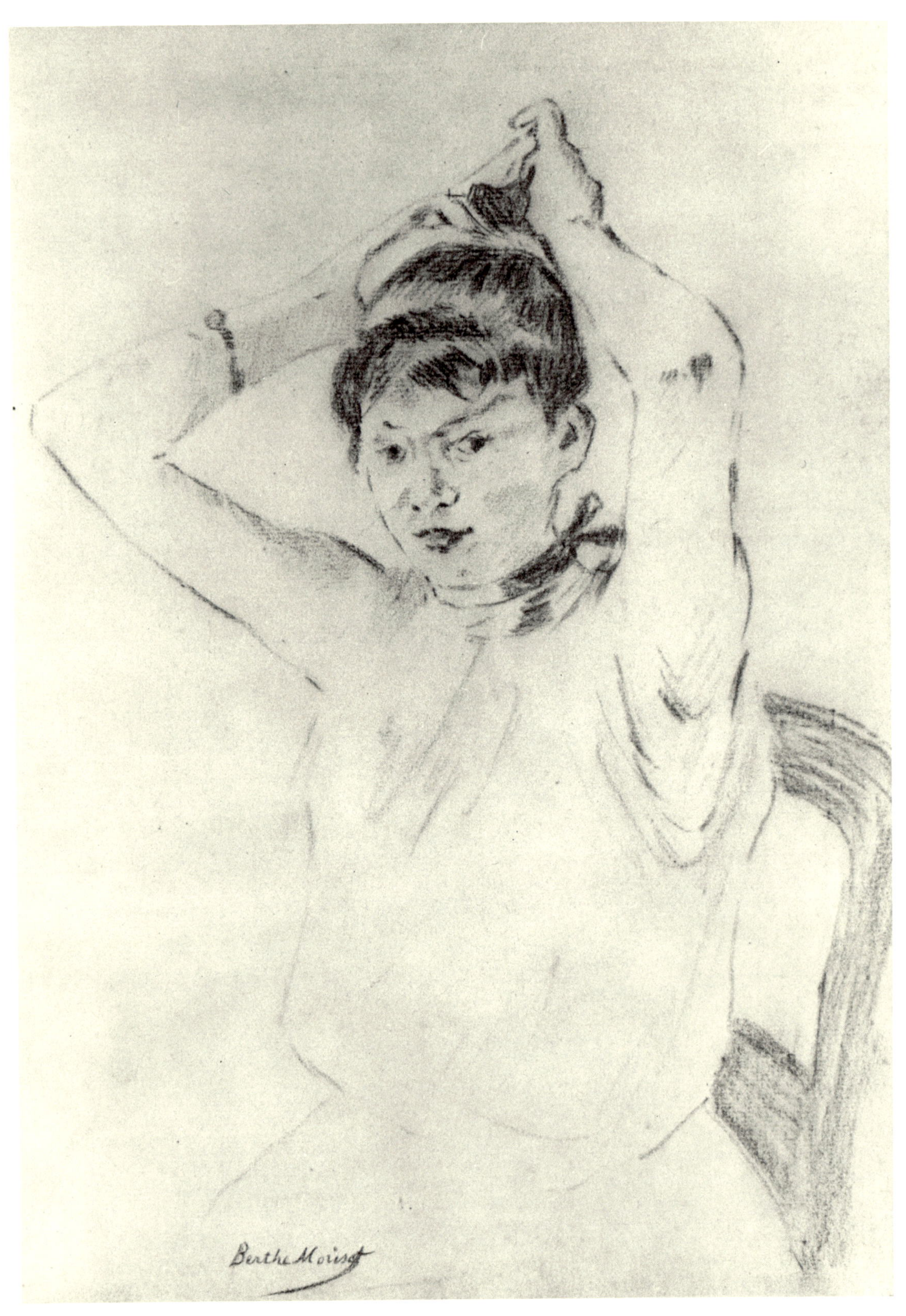

20 Berthe Morisot. *Woman Dressing Her Hair*

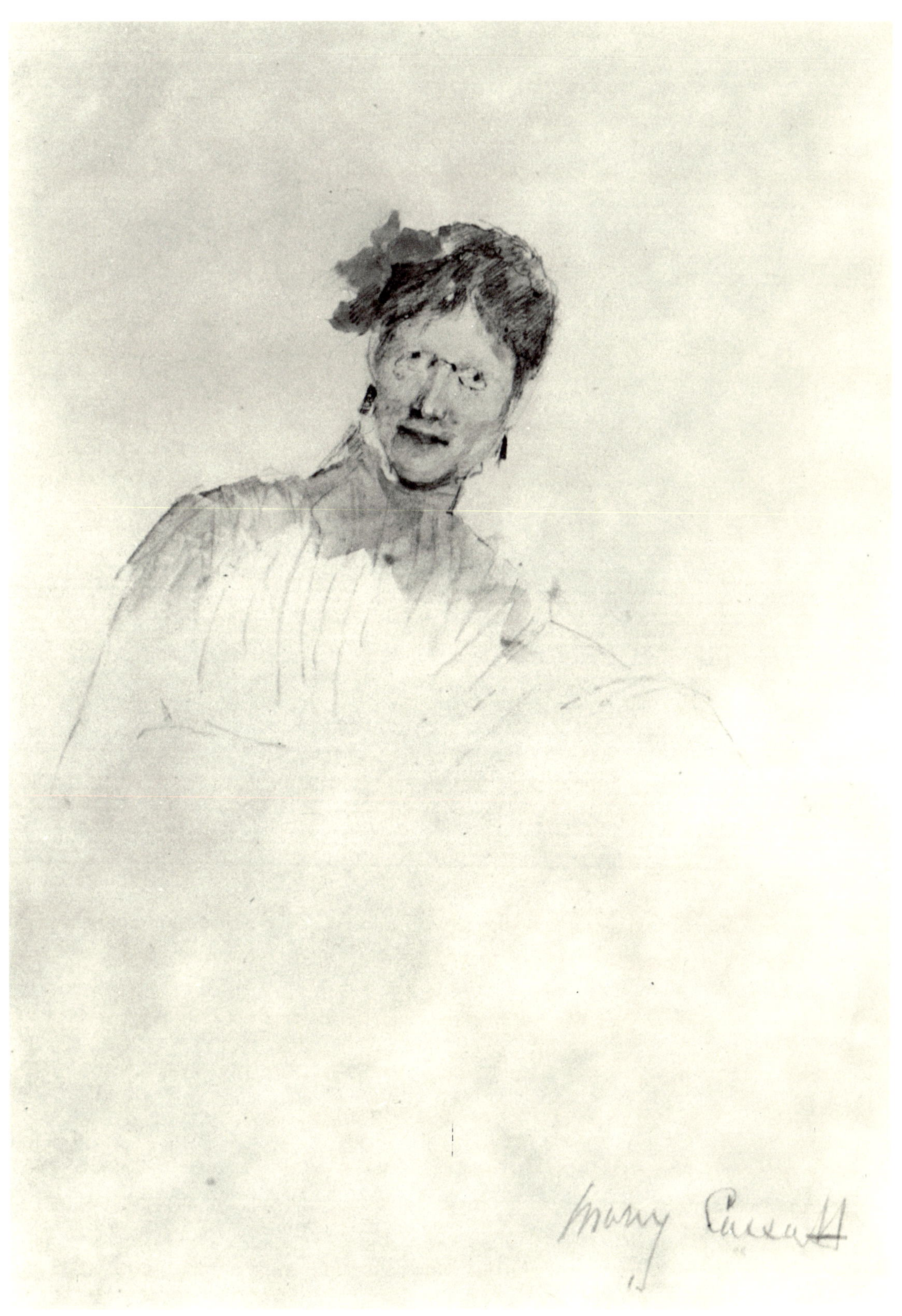

21 Mary Cassatt. *Vernon Lee*

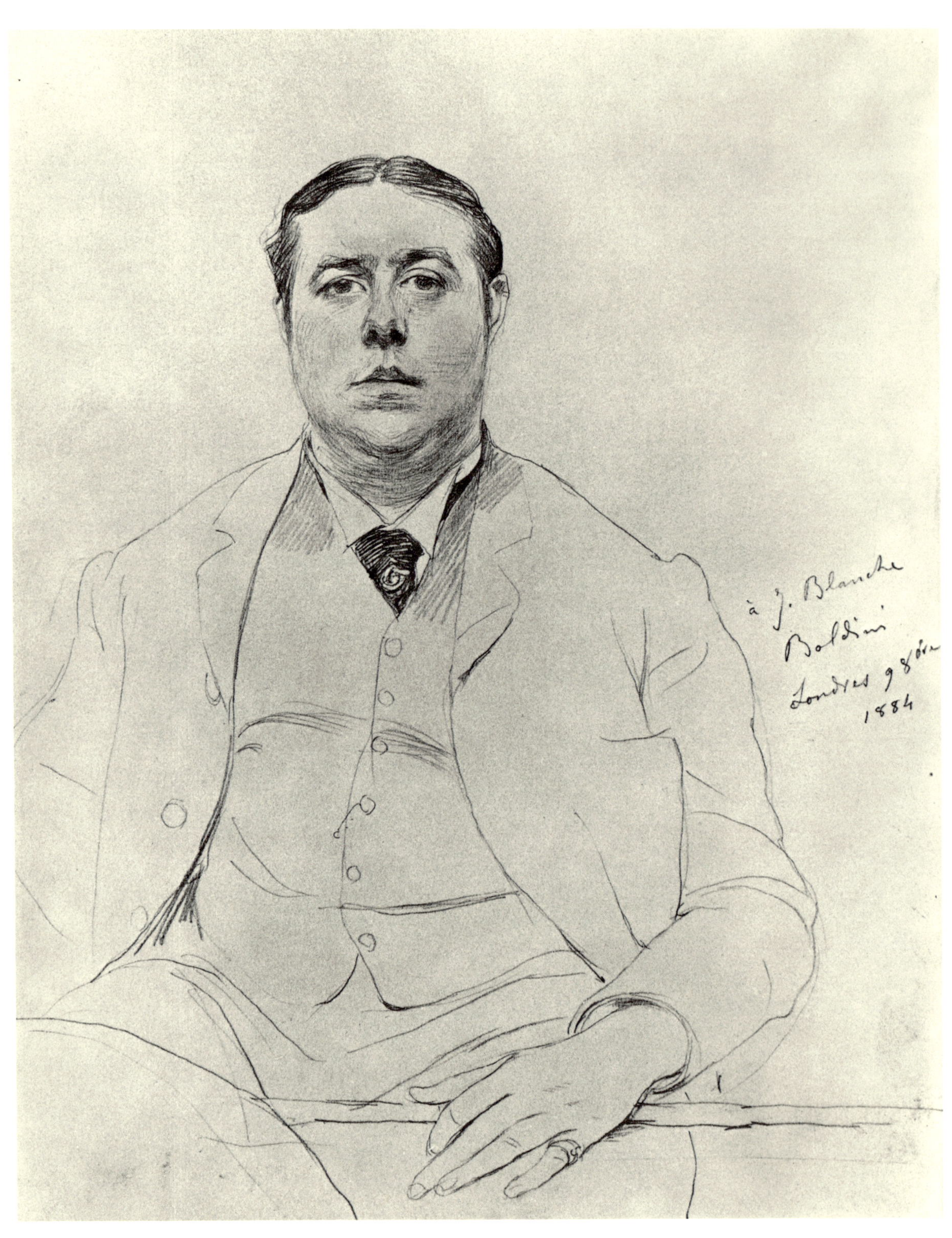

22 Giovanni Boldini. *Jacques-Émile Blanche*

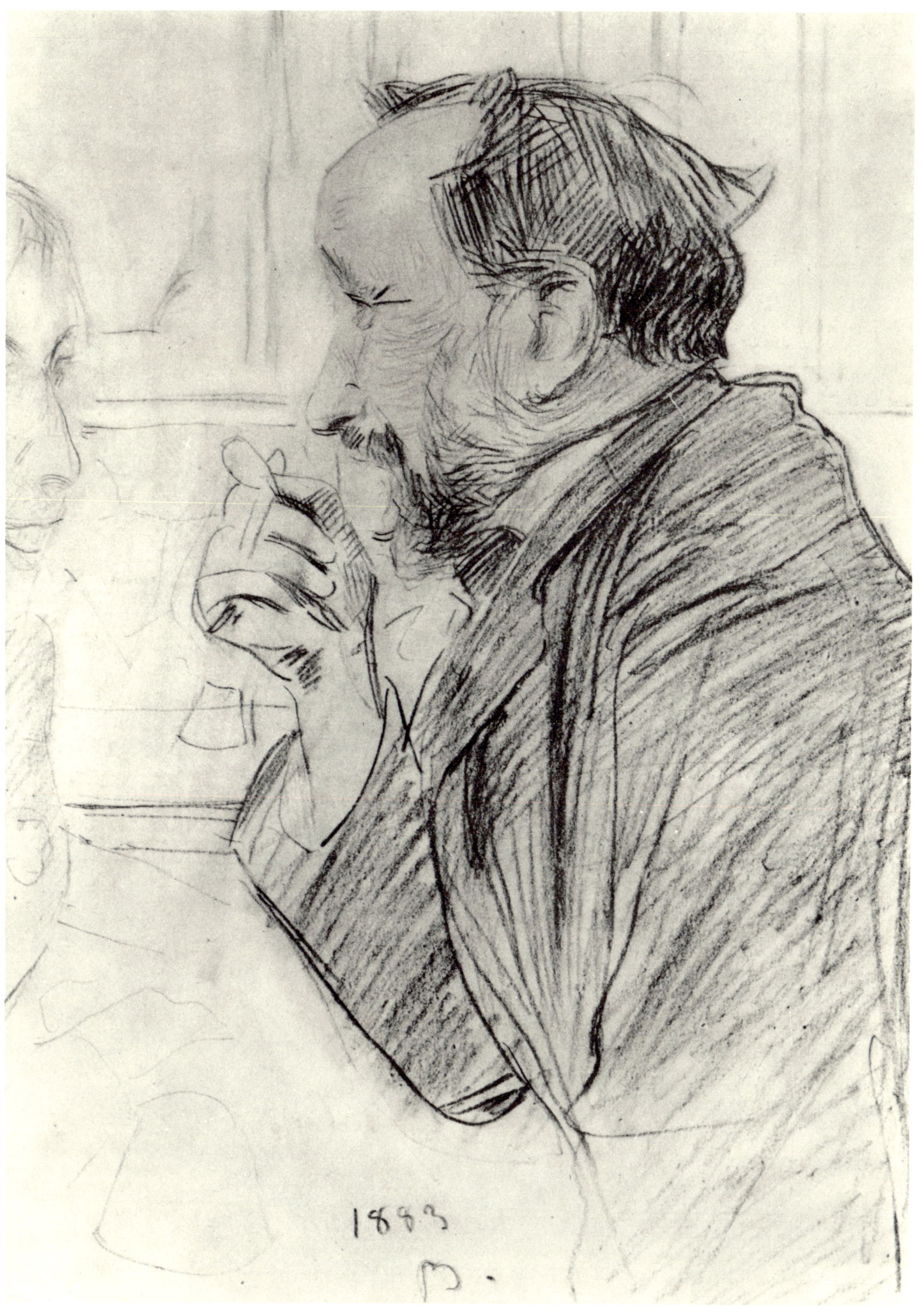

23 Giovanni Boldini. *Edgar Degas*

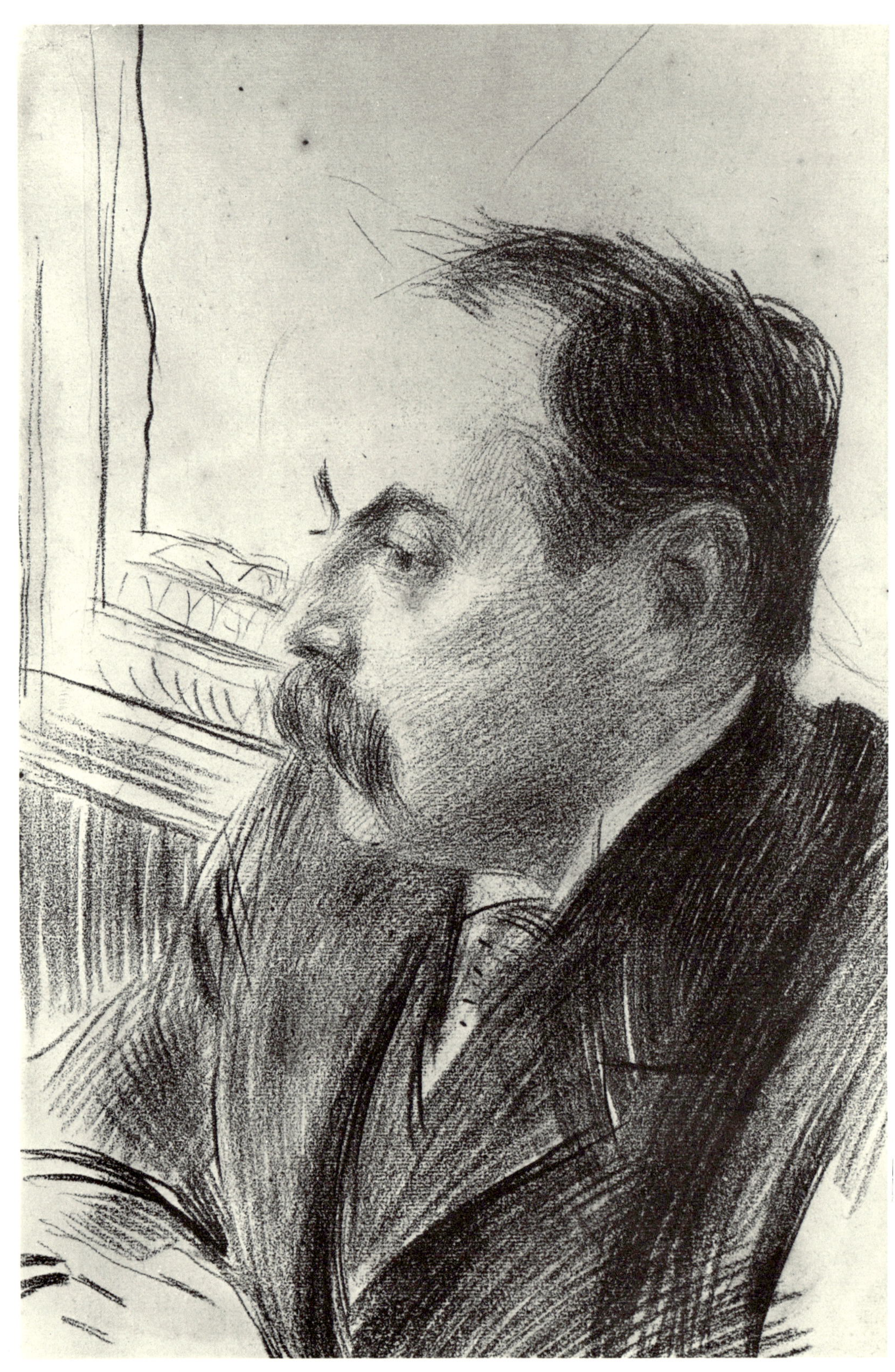

24 Giovanni Boldini. *Le Marquis de Biron*

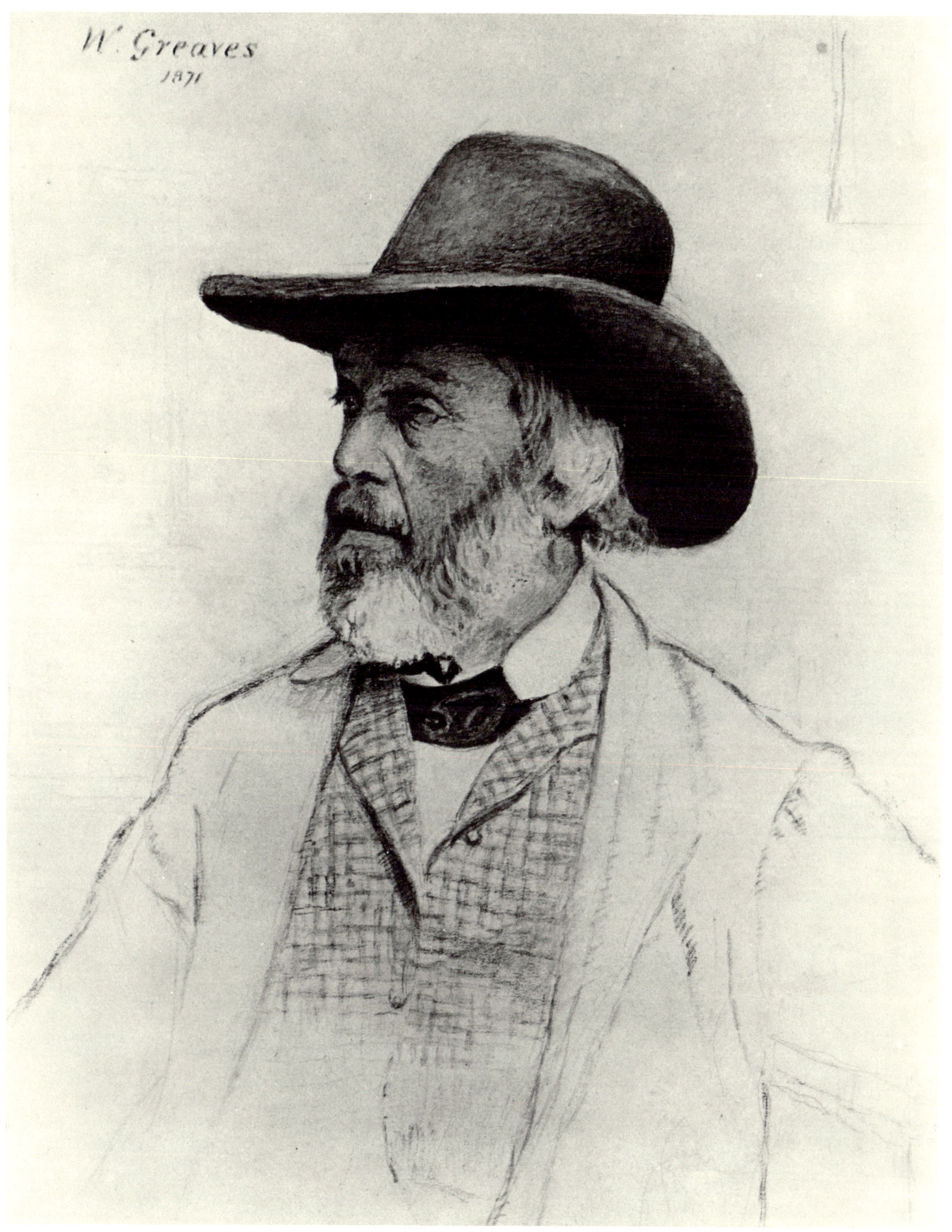

25 Walter Greaves. *Thomas Carlyle*

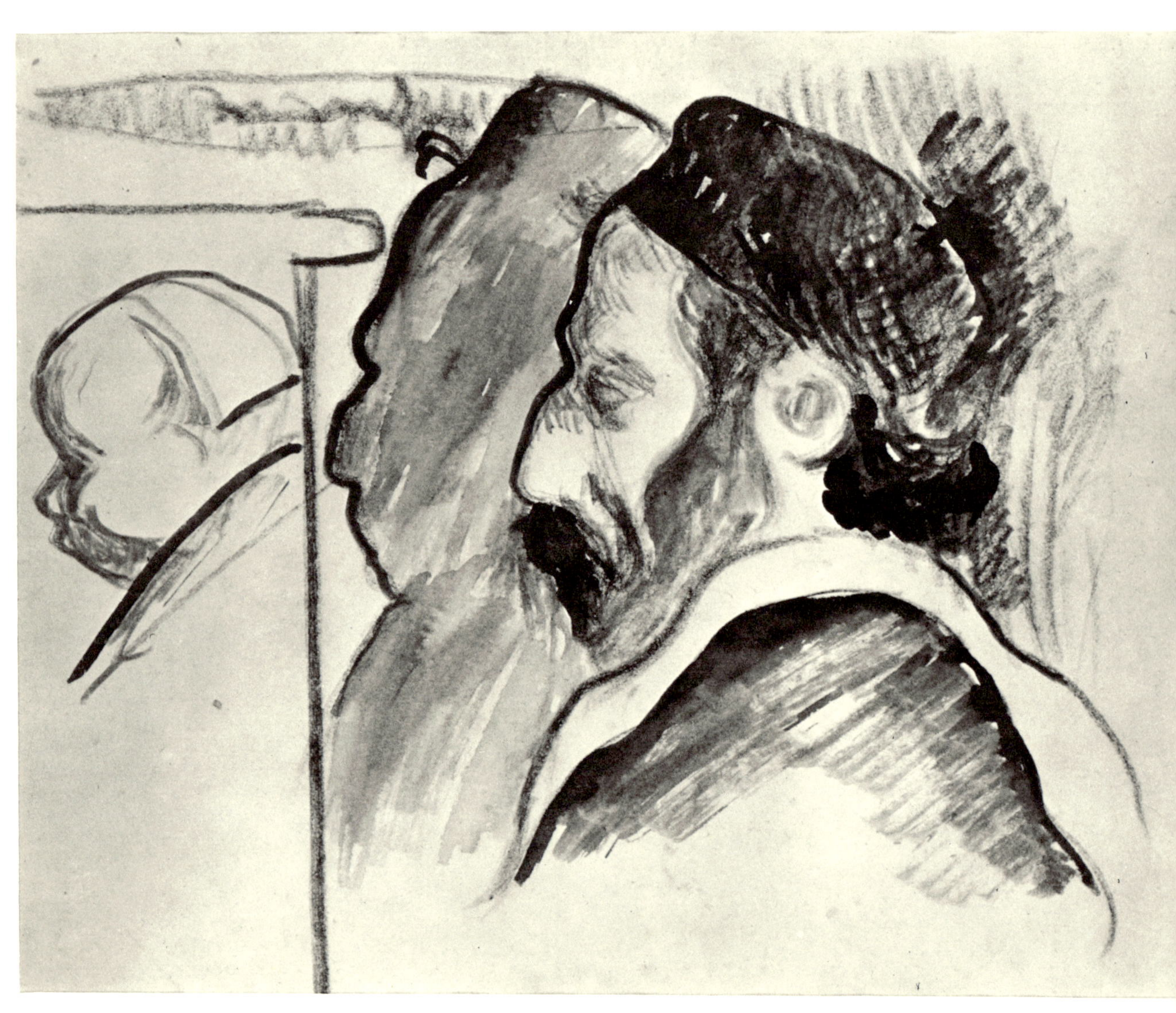

26 Paul Gauguin. *Man in a Skullcap and Head of Mimi*

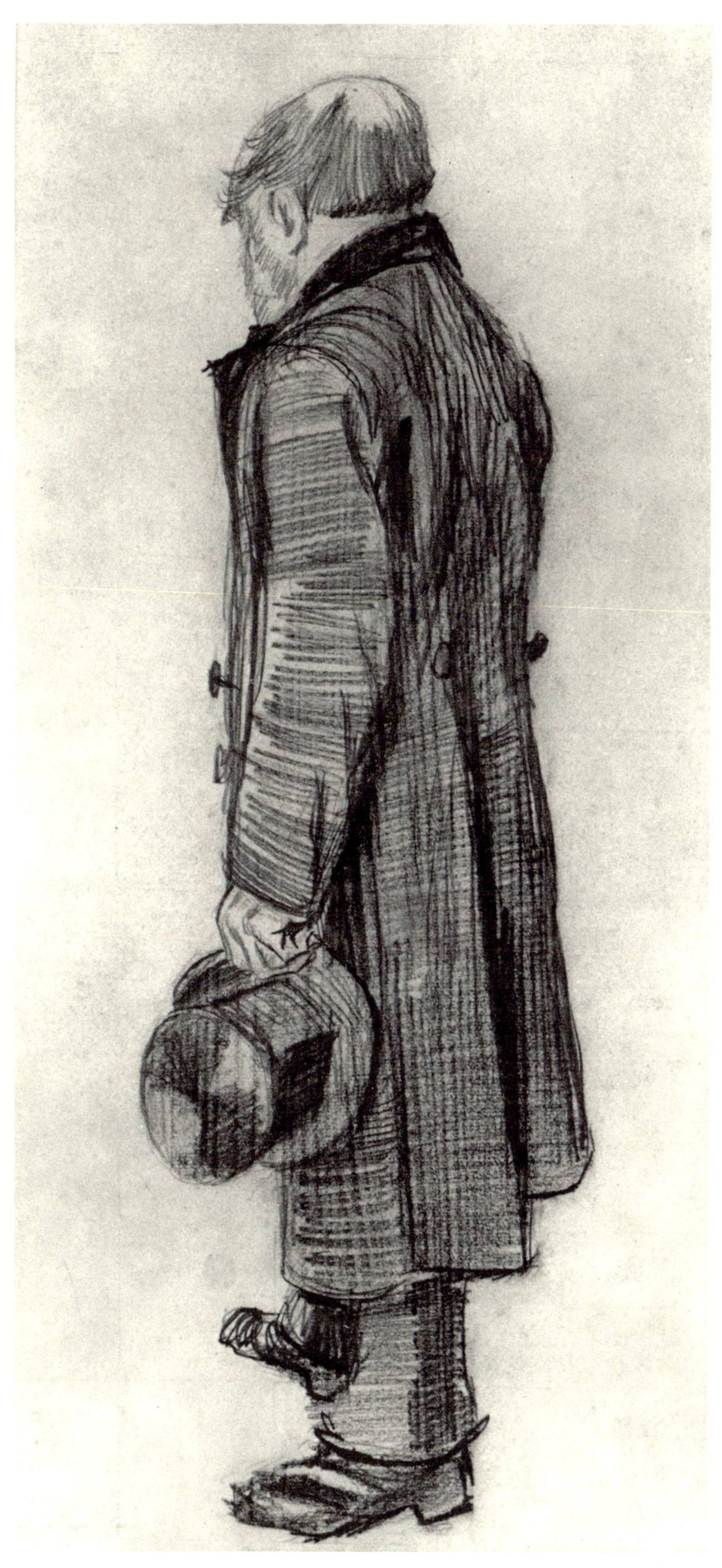

27 Vincent van Gogh. *Man Standing, Hat in Hand*

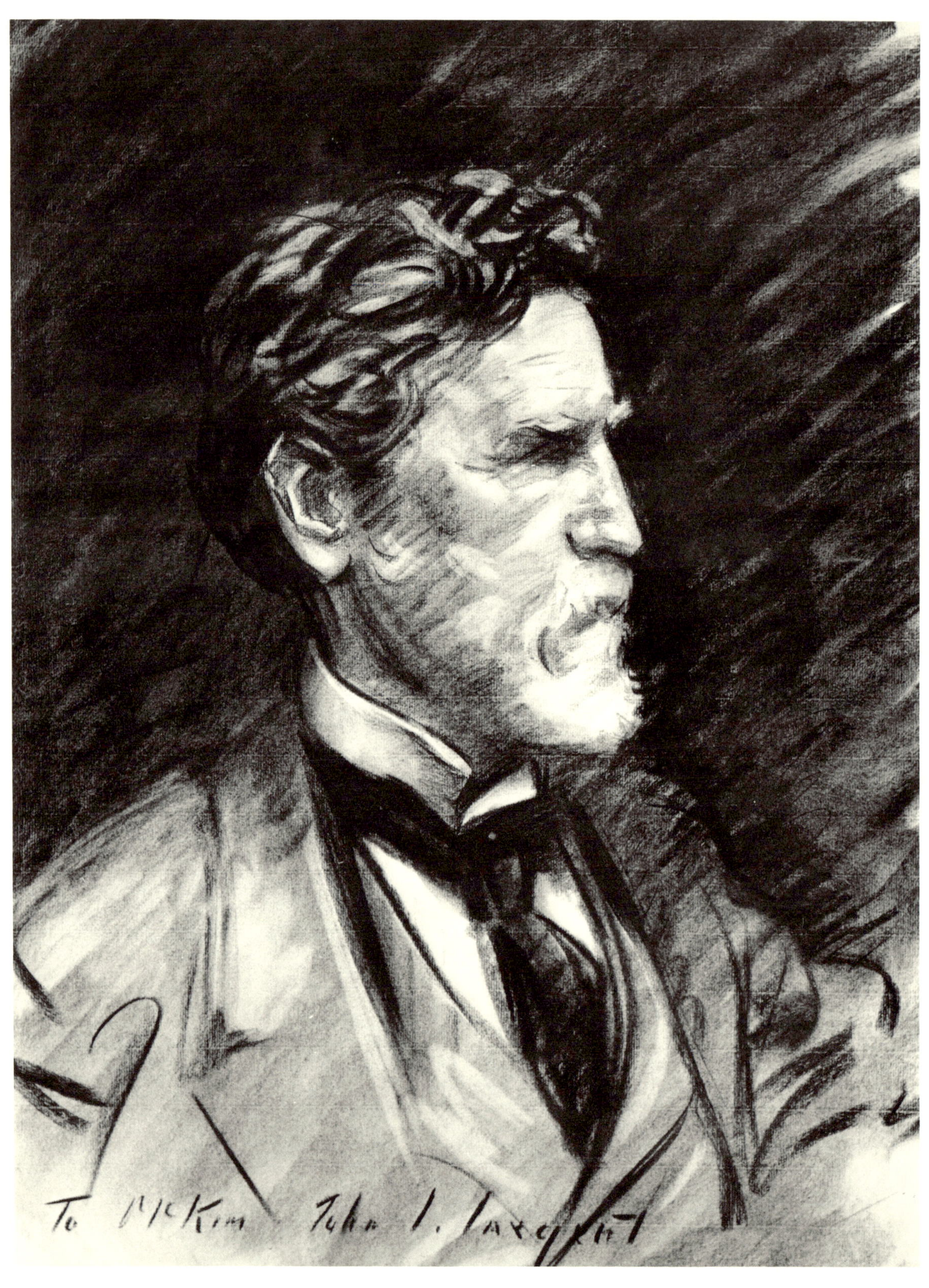

28 John Singer Sargent. *Augustus Saint-Gaudens*

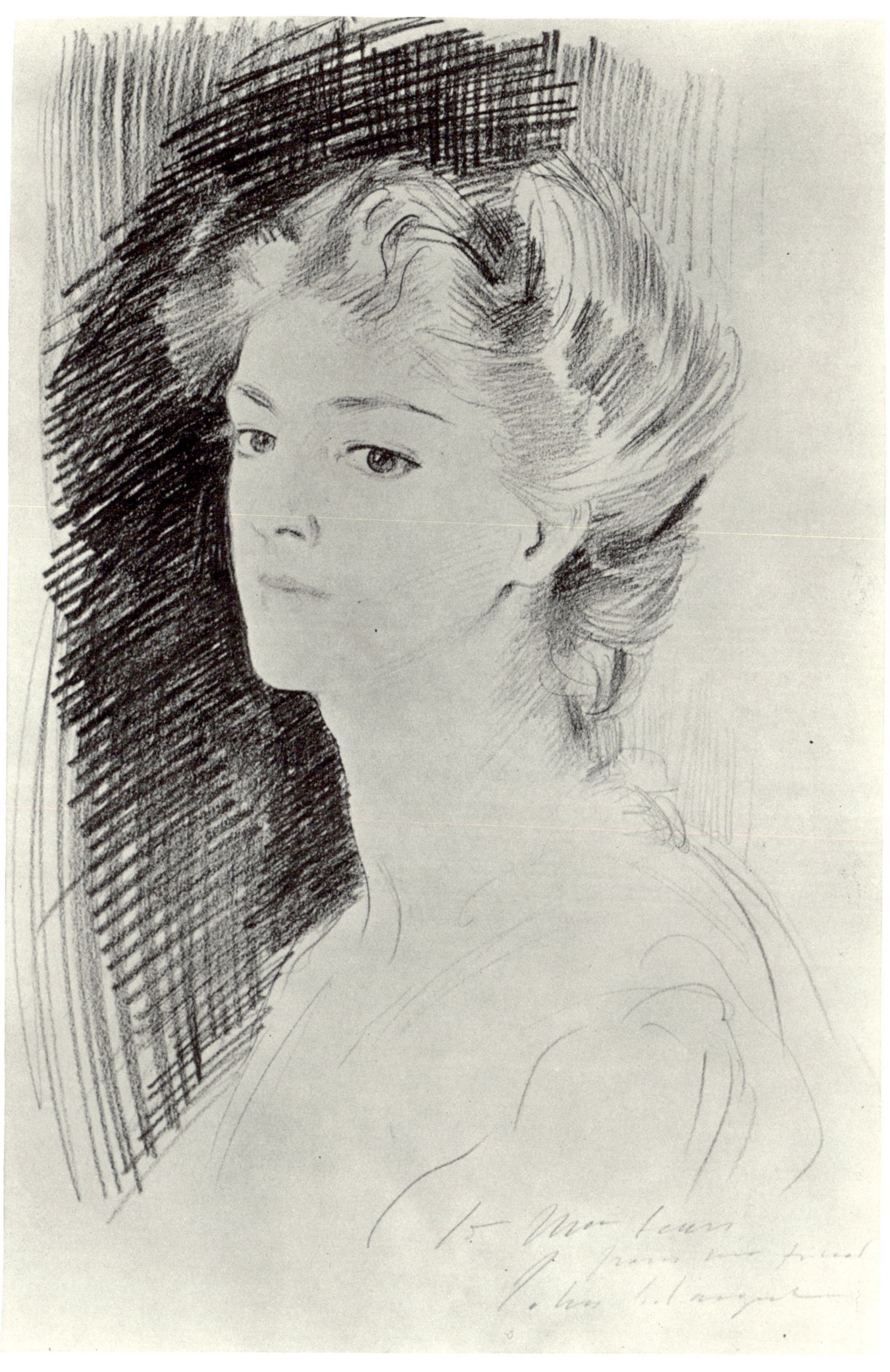

29 John Singer Sargent. *Ethel Barrymore*

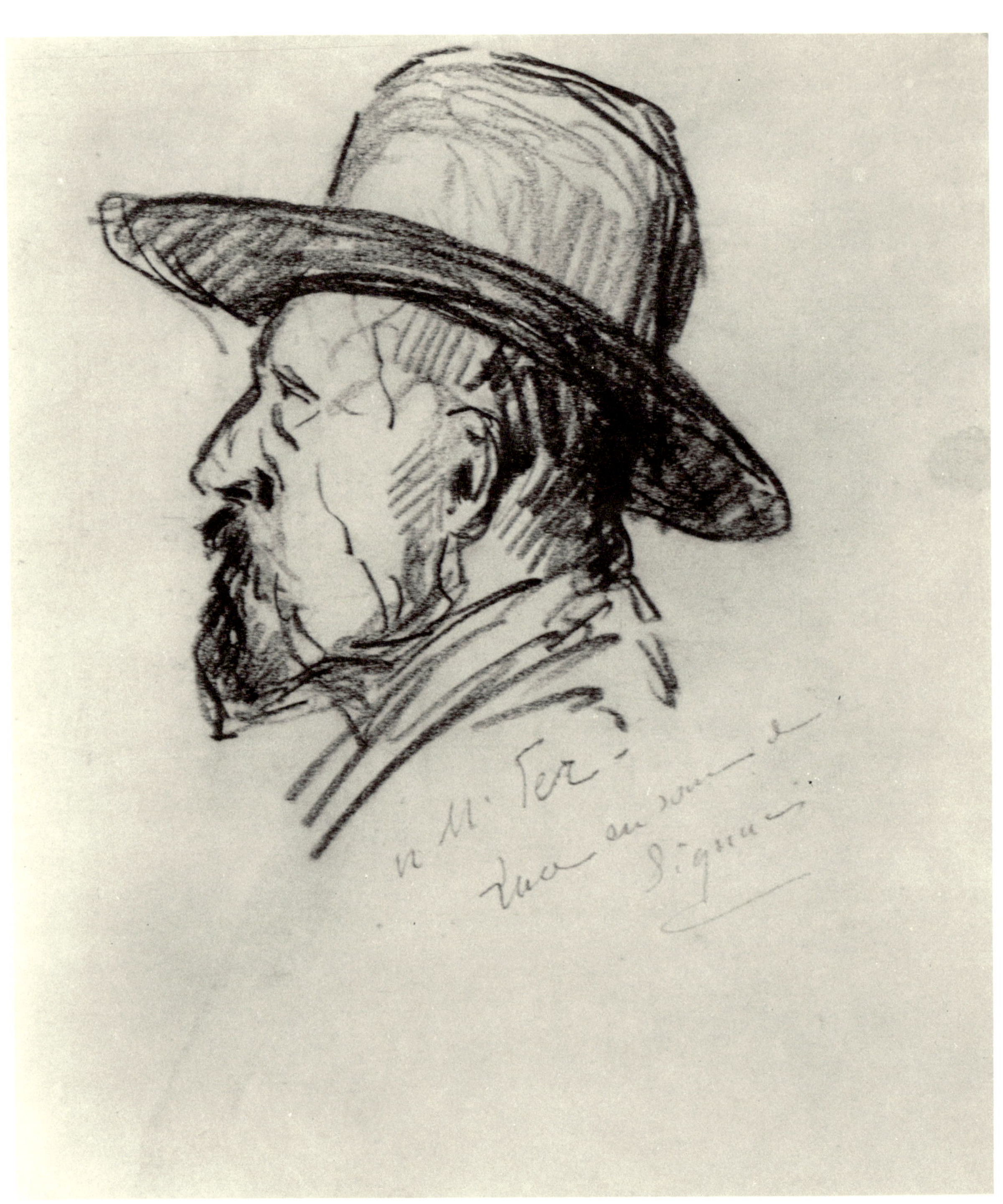

30 Maximilien Luce. *Paul Signac*

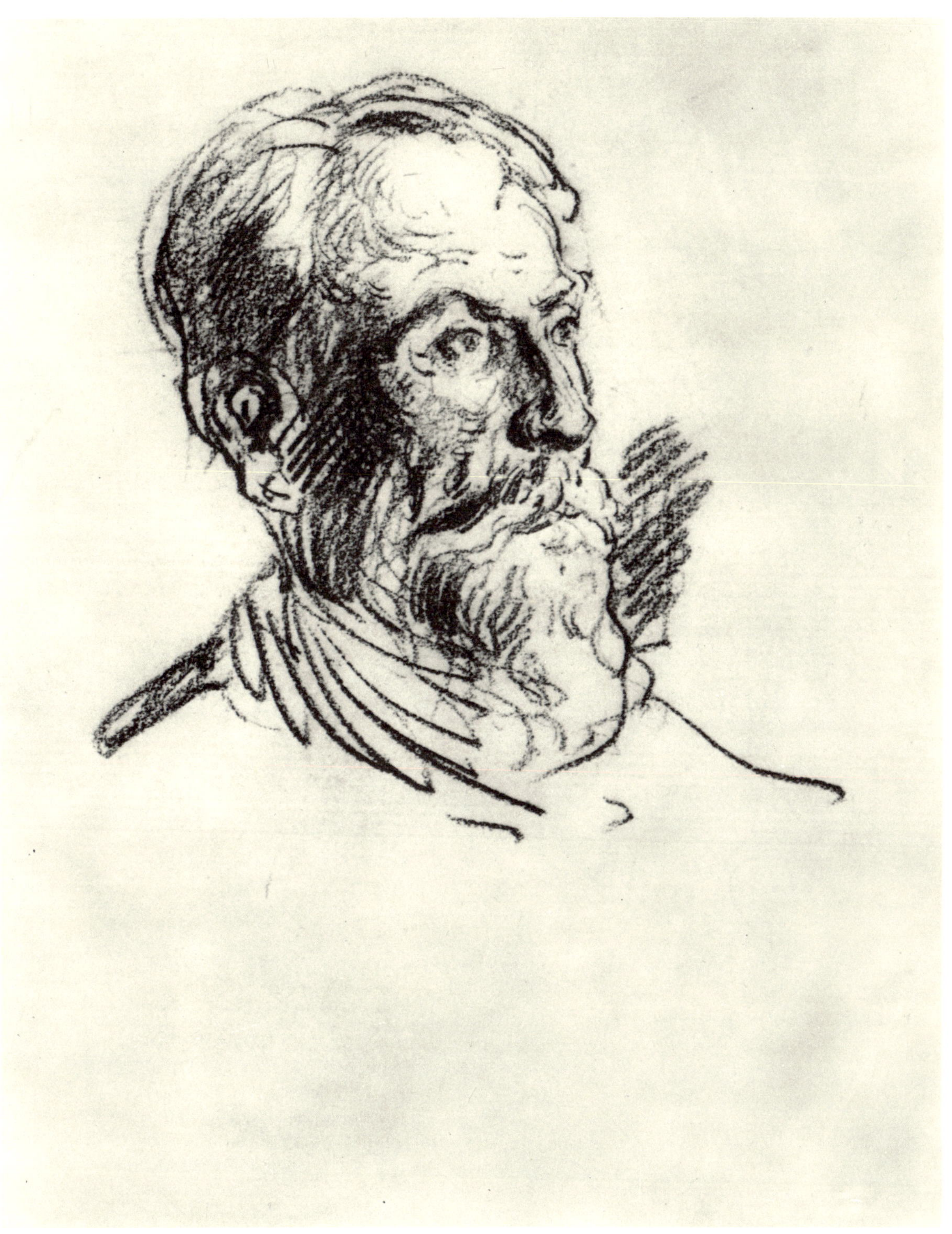

31 Maximilien Luce. *Henry E. Cross*

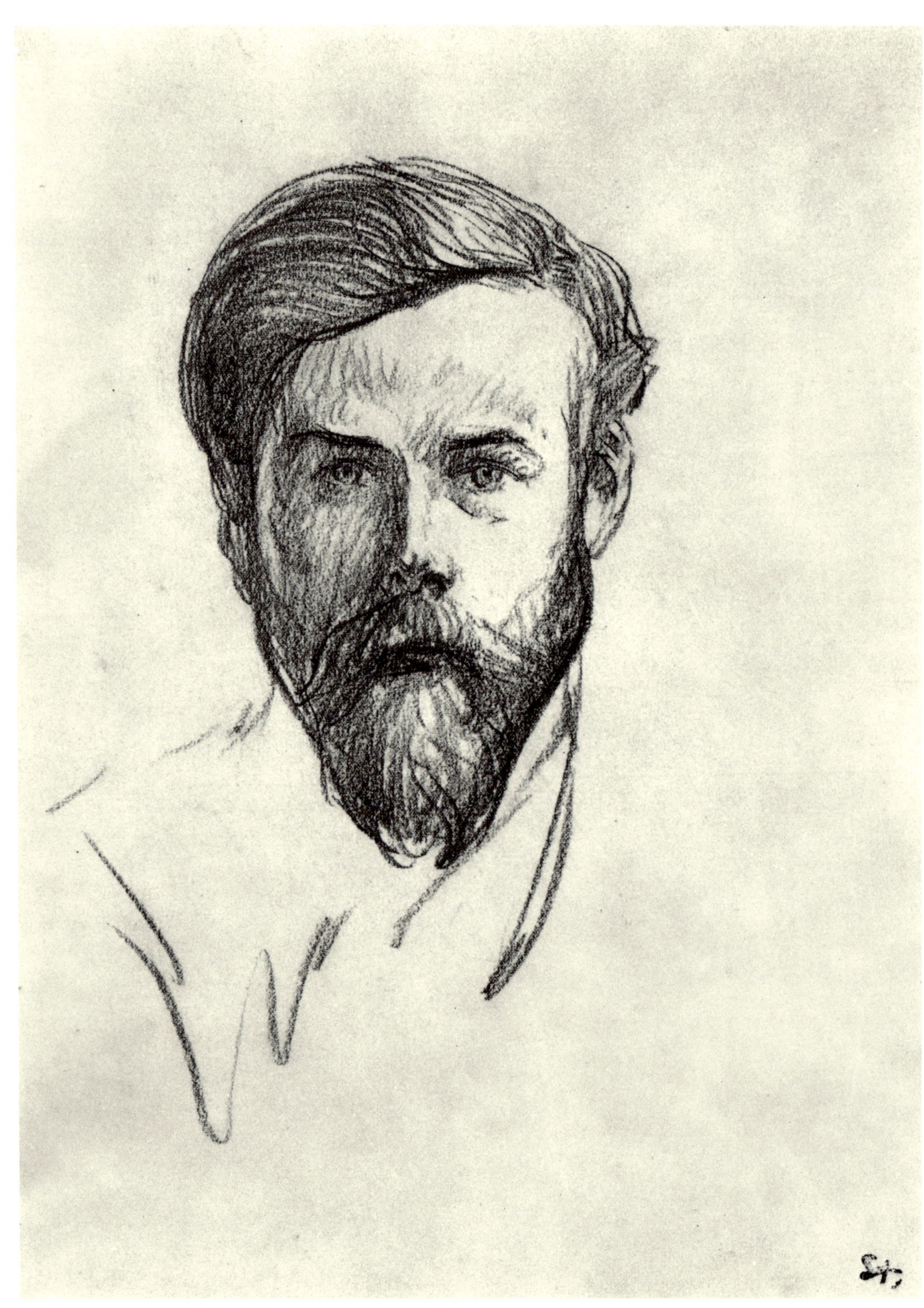

32 Théophile-Alexandre Steinlen. *Claude Debussy*

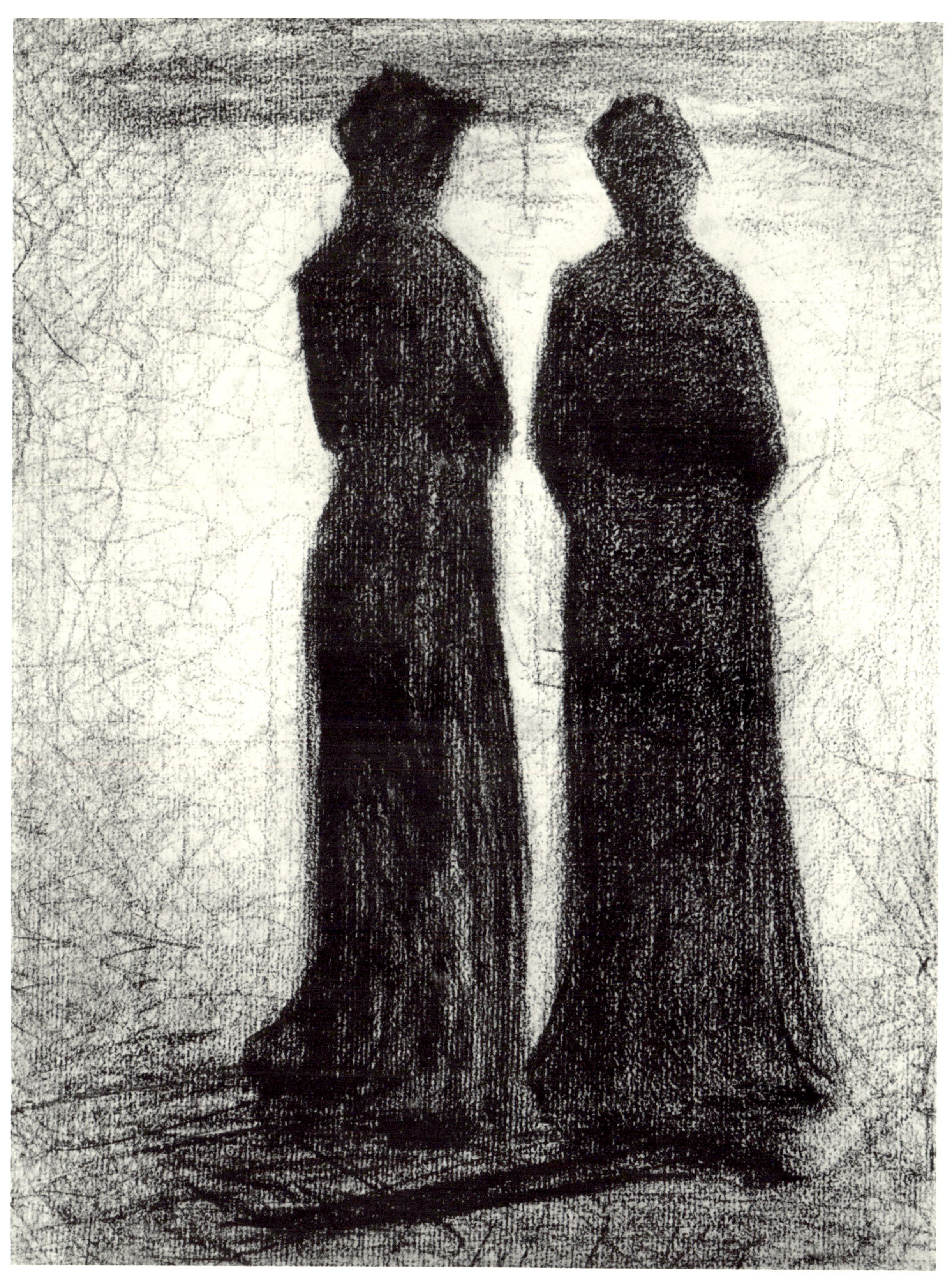

33 Georges-Pierre Seurat. *Mme Appert and Mme Seurat*

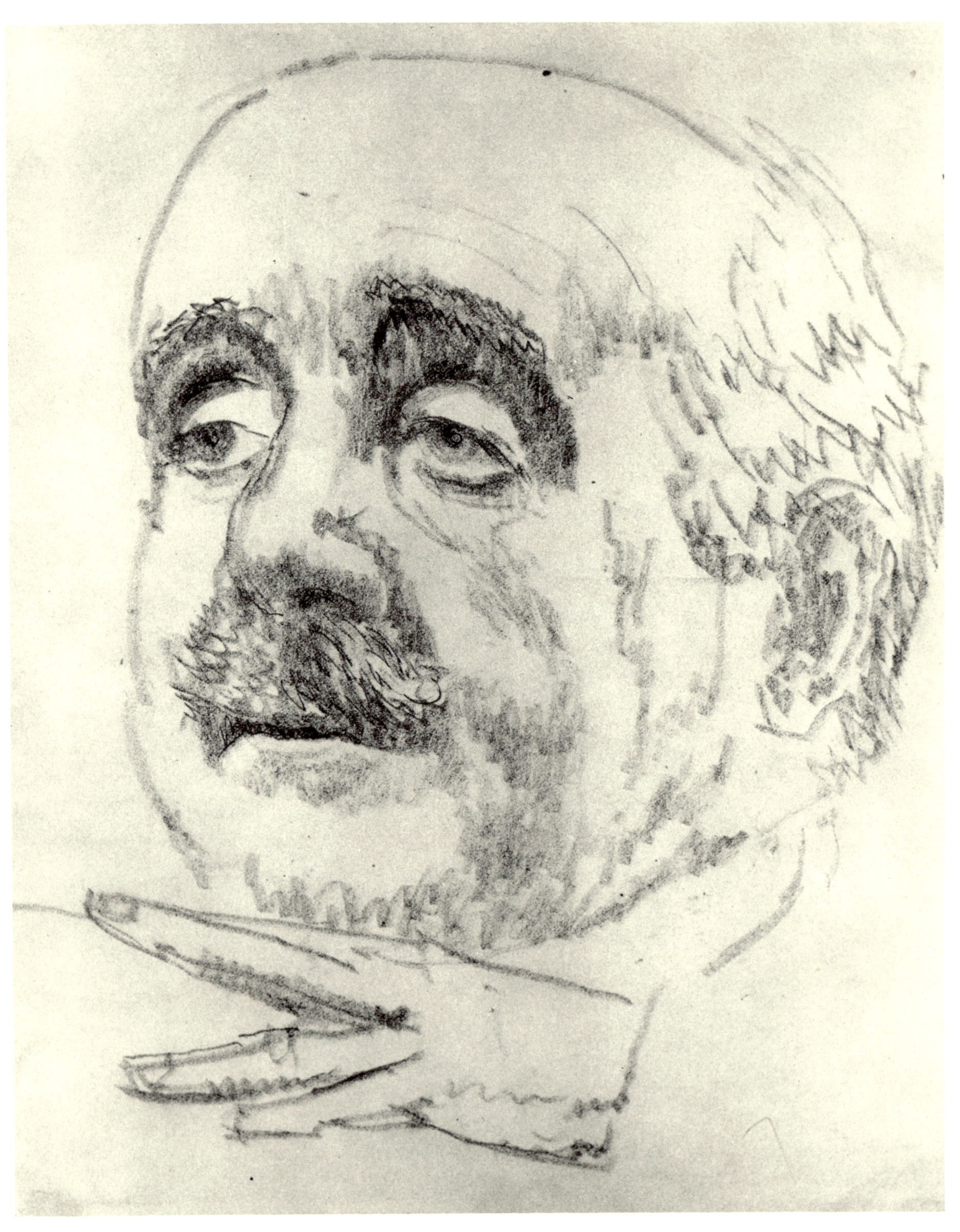

34 Walter Richard Sickert. *Sir Max Beerbohm*

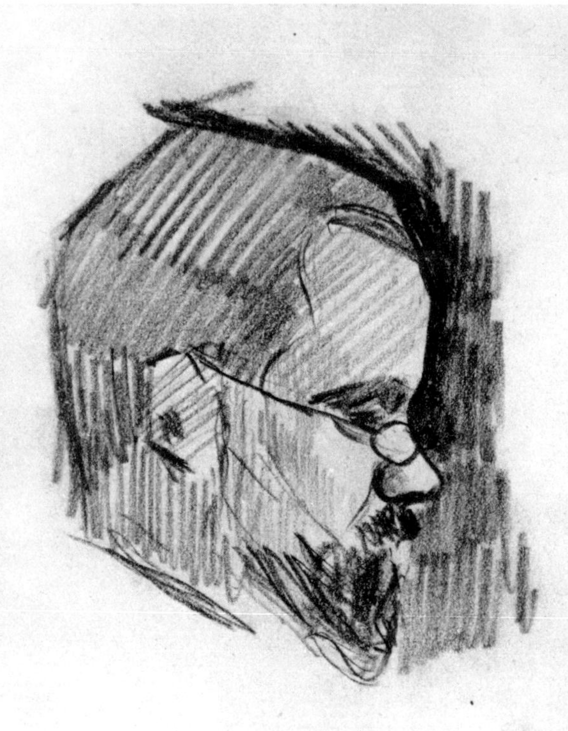

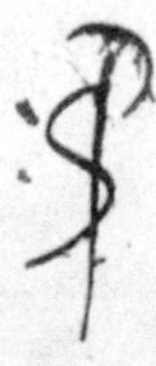

35 Paul Signac. *Maximilien Luce*

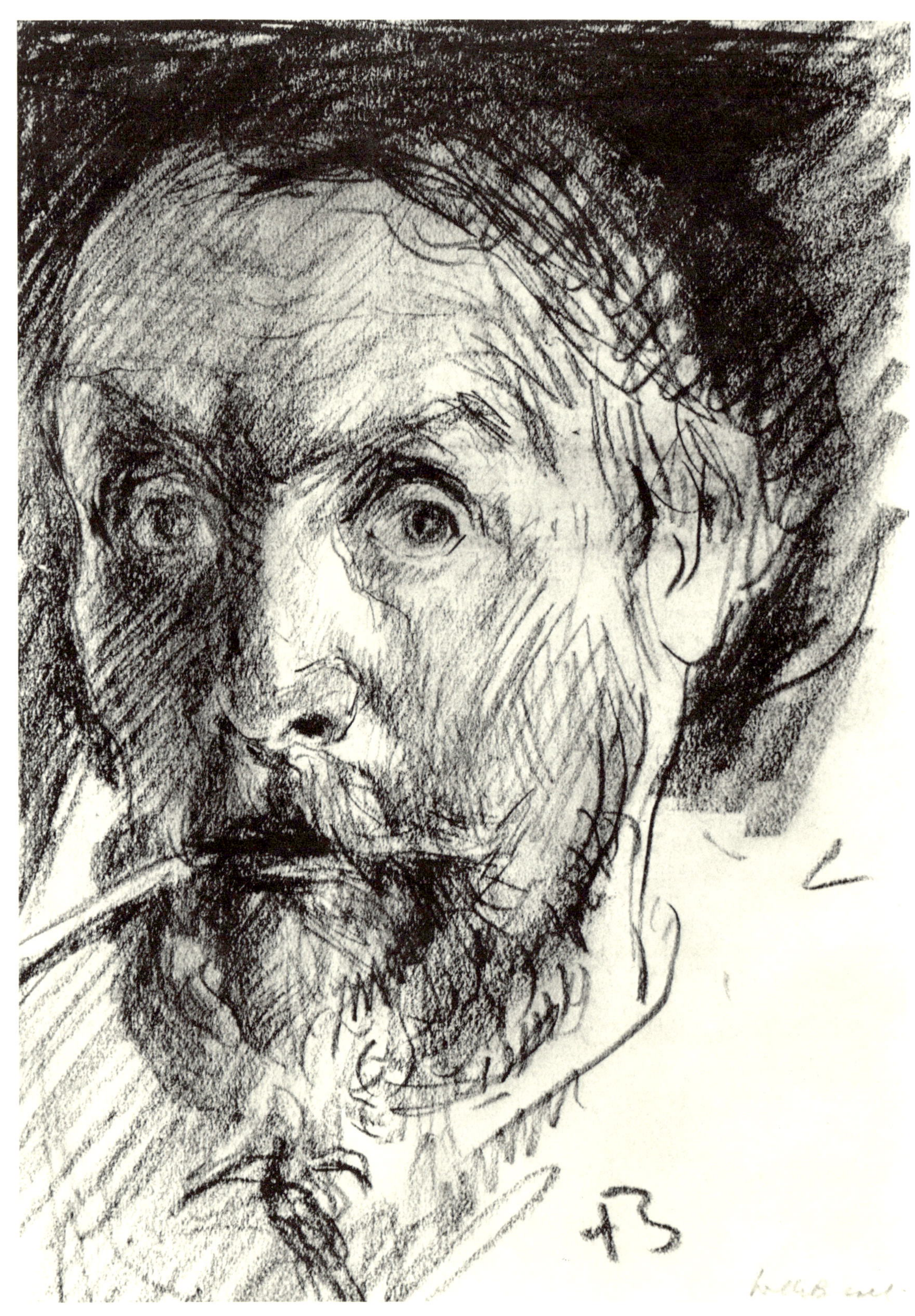

36 Sir Frank Brangwyn. *Self-Portrait*

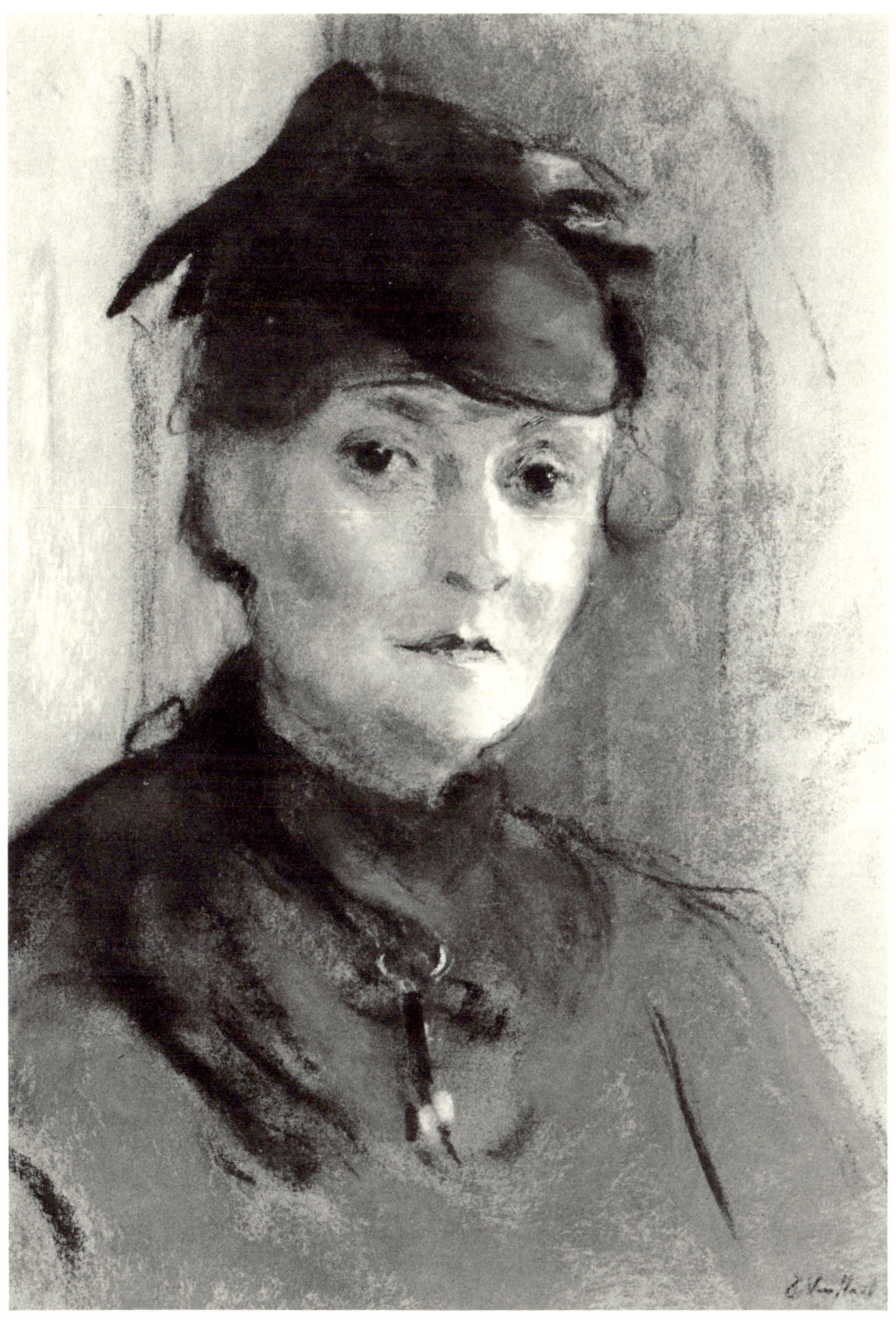

37 Édouard Vuillard. *The Princess Bibesco*

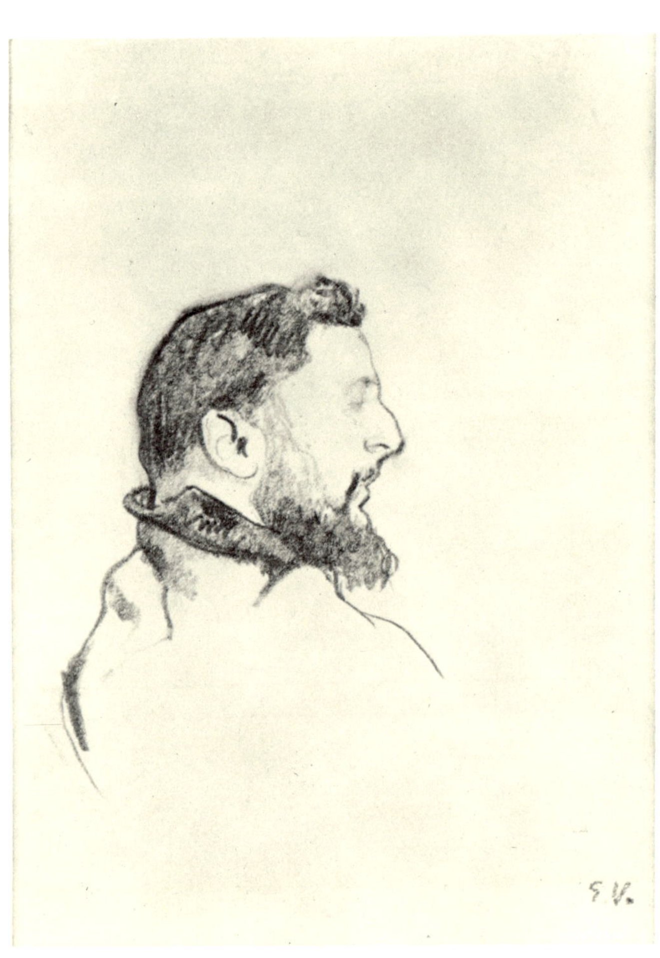

38 Édouard Vuillard. *Thadée Natanson*

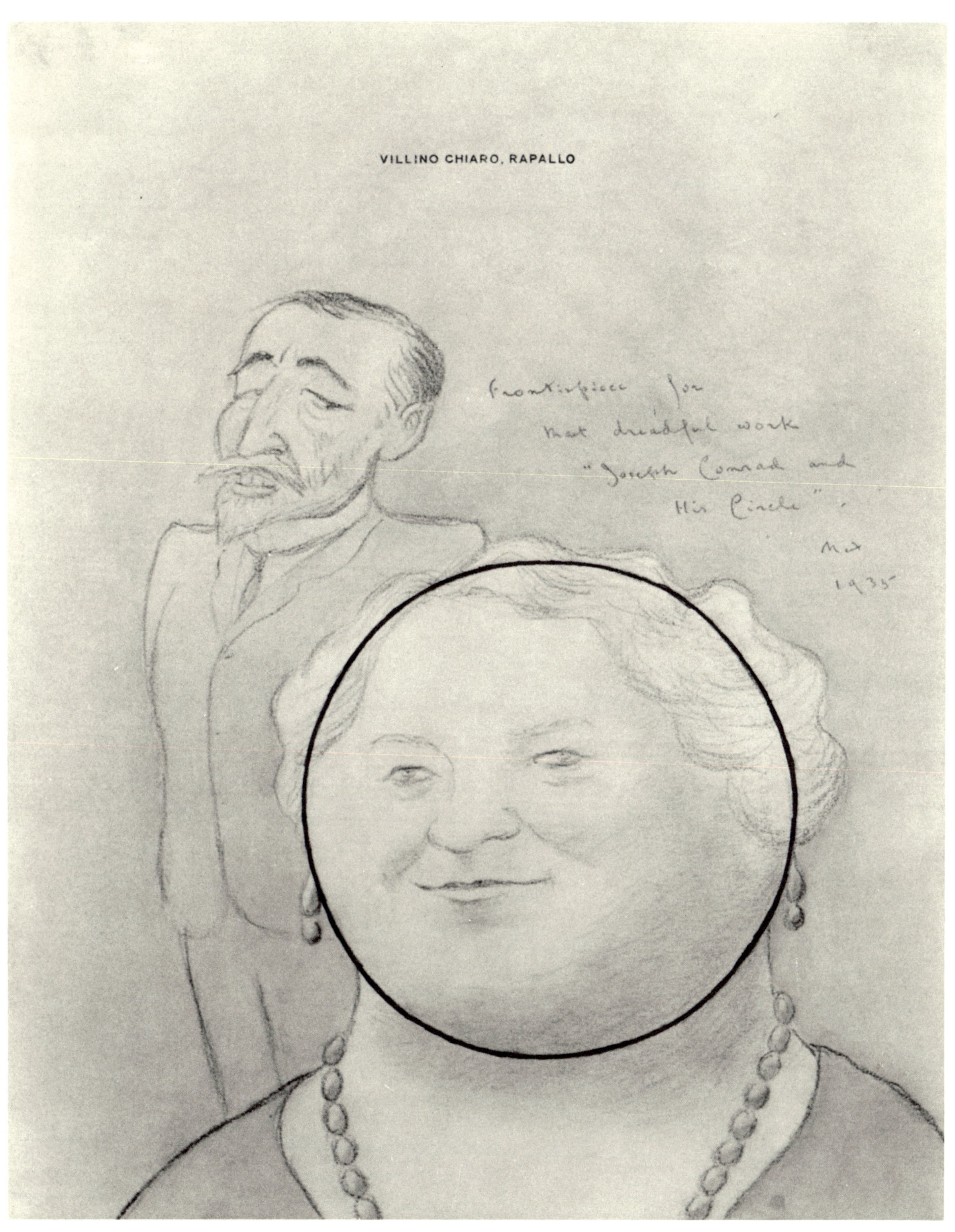

39 Sir Max Beerbohm. *"Joseph Conrad and His Circle"*

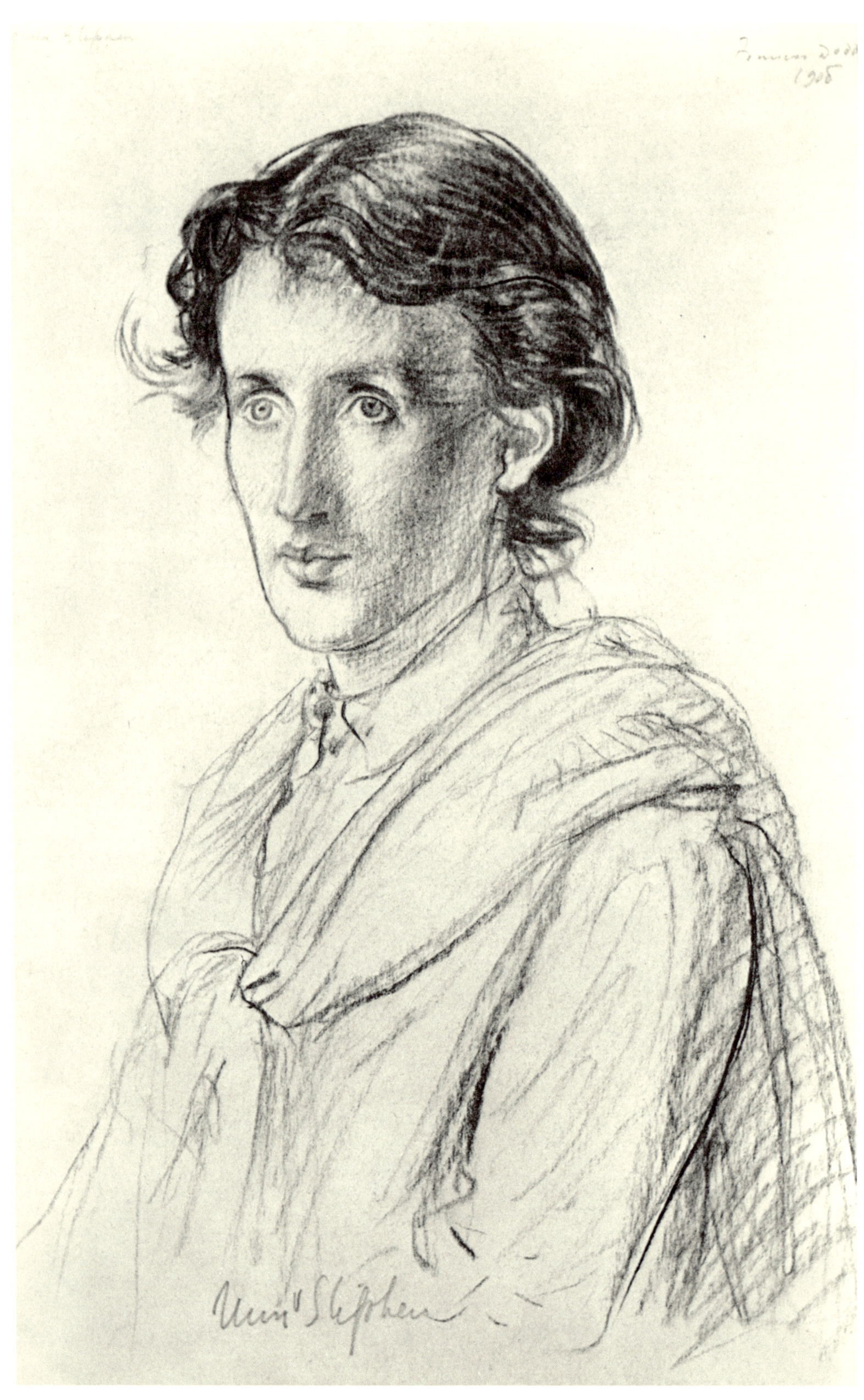

40 Francis Dodd. *Virginia Woolf*

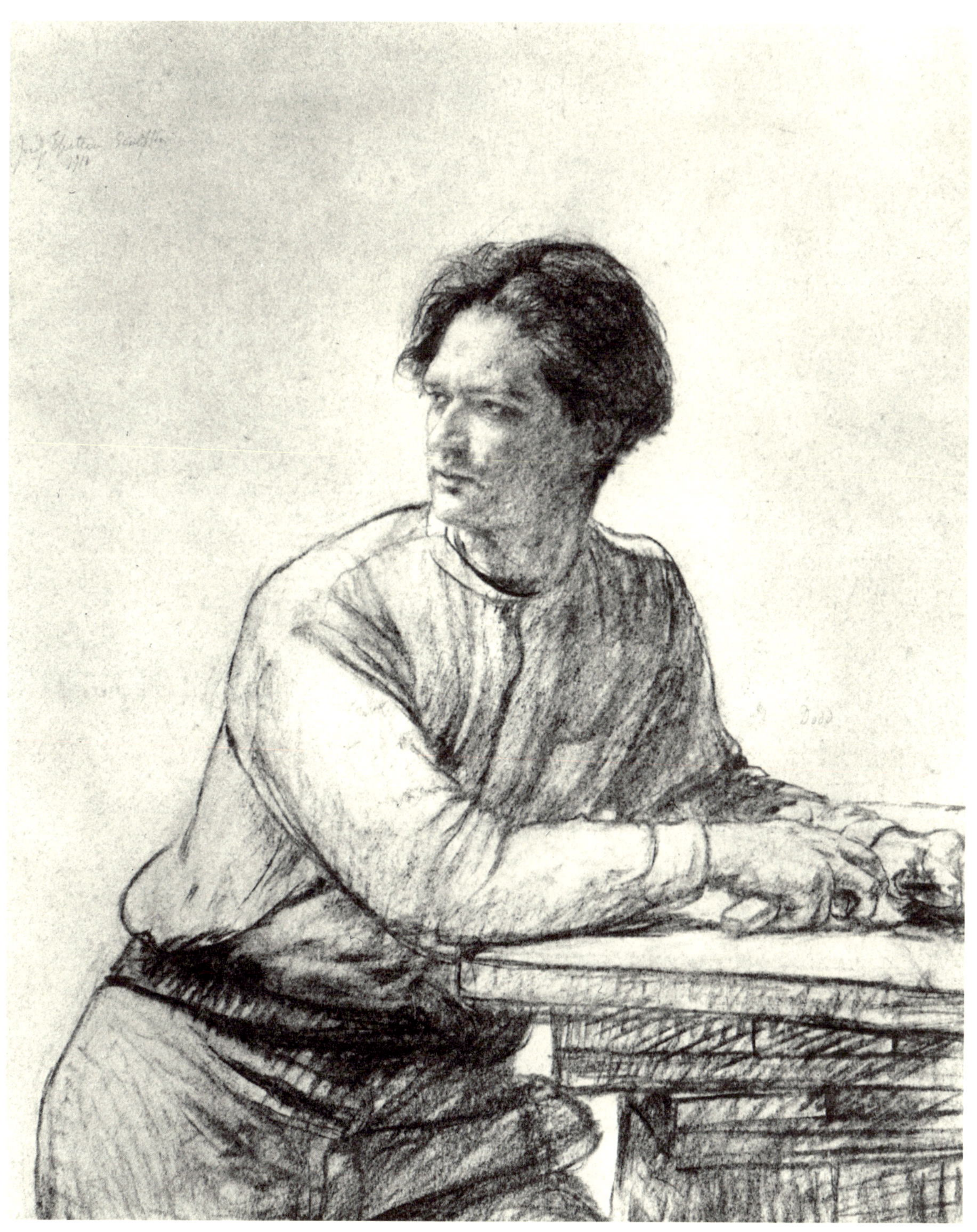

41 Francis Dodd. *Sir Jacob Epstein*

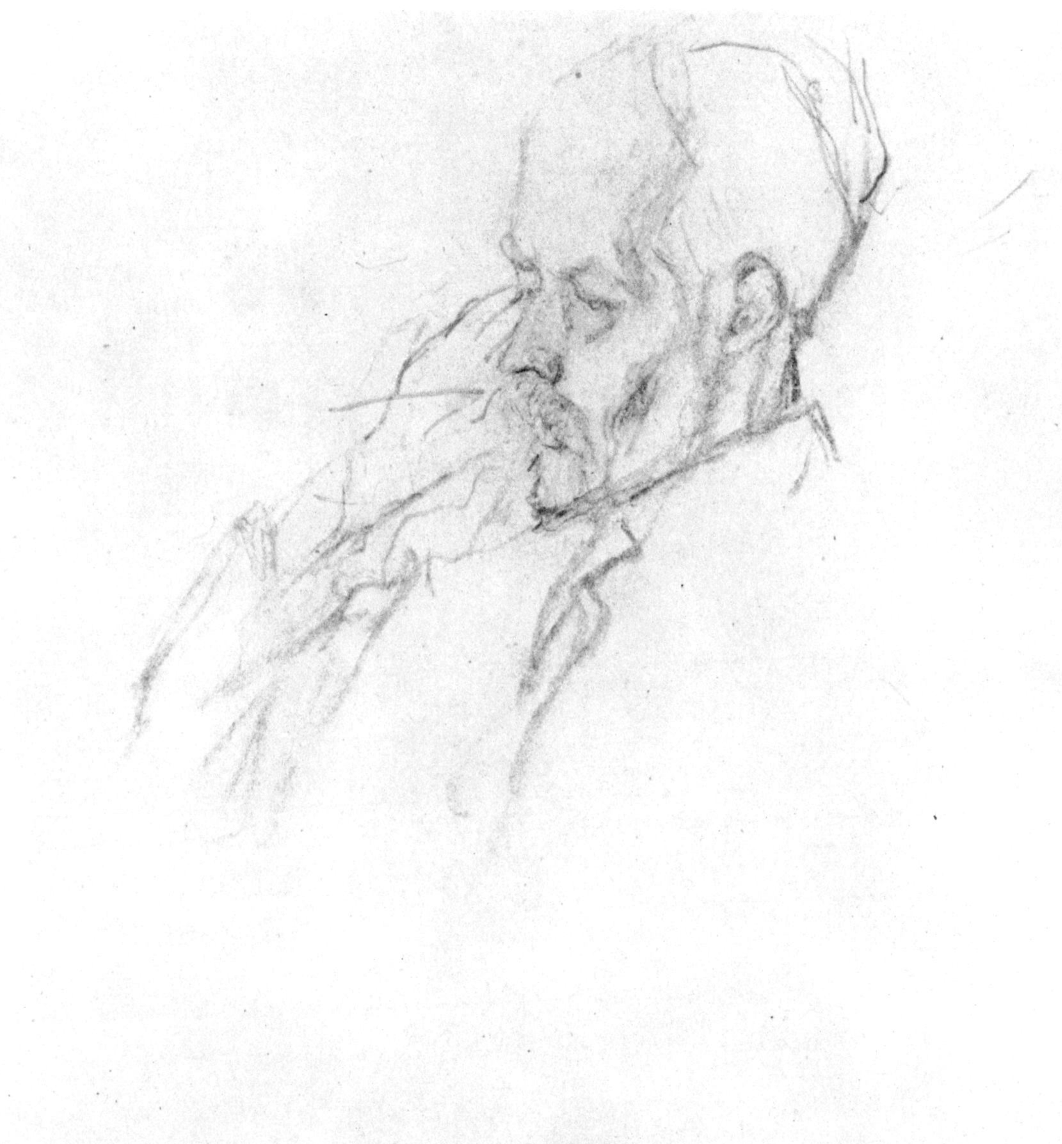

42 Gwen John. *Arthur Symons*

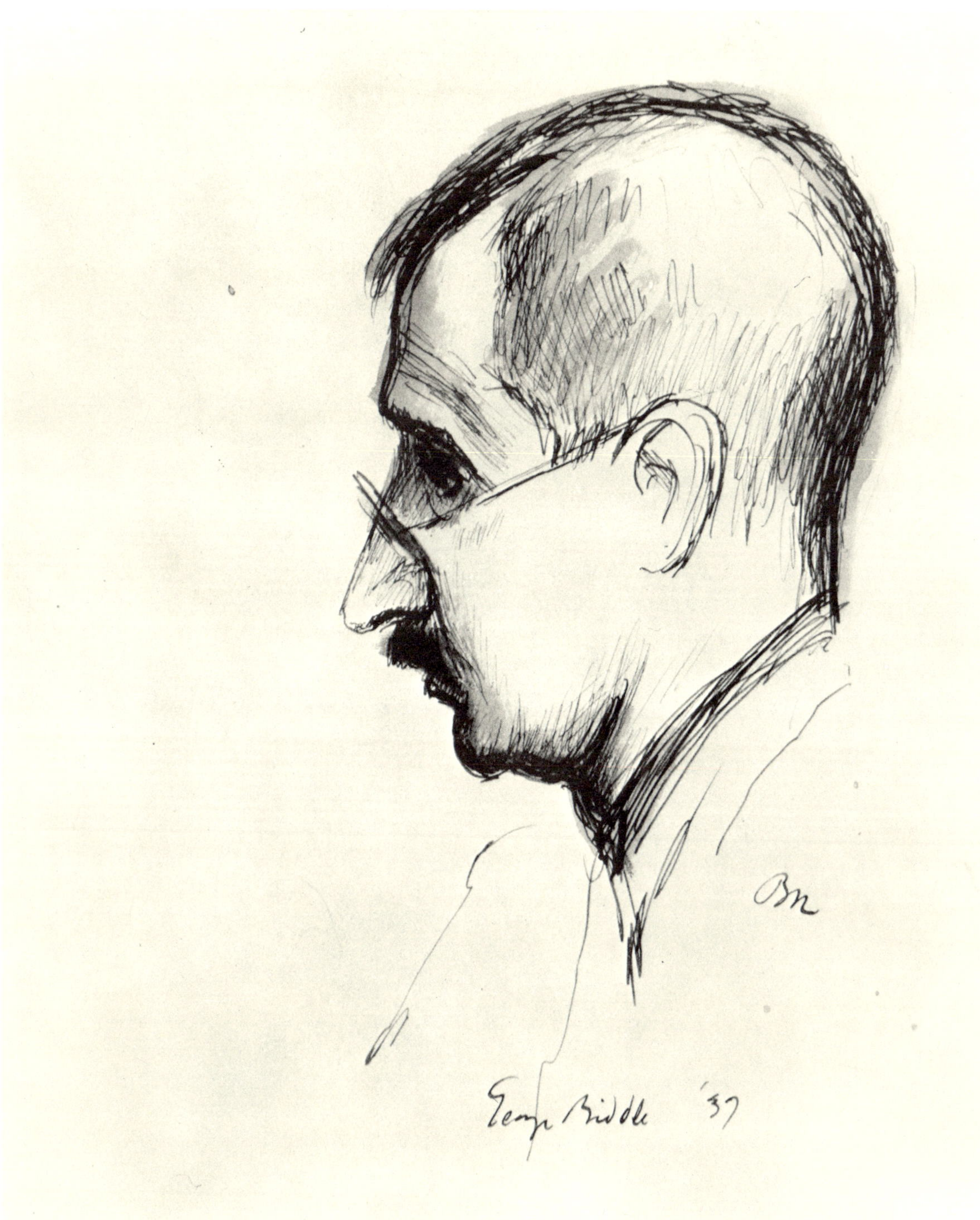

43 Boardman Robinson. *George Biddle*

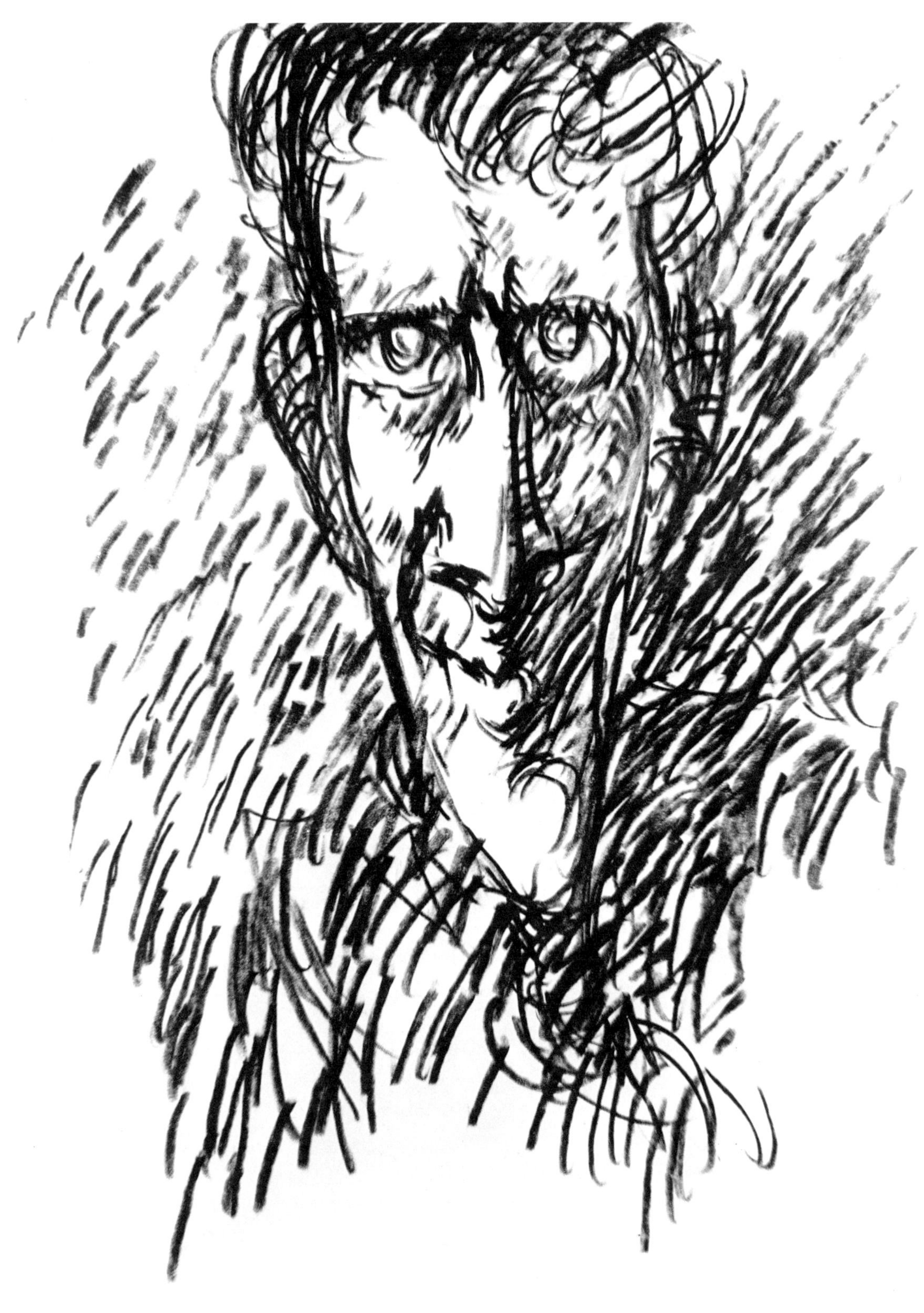

44 Marsden Hartley. *Self-Portrait*

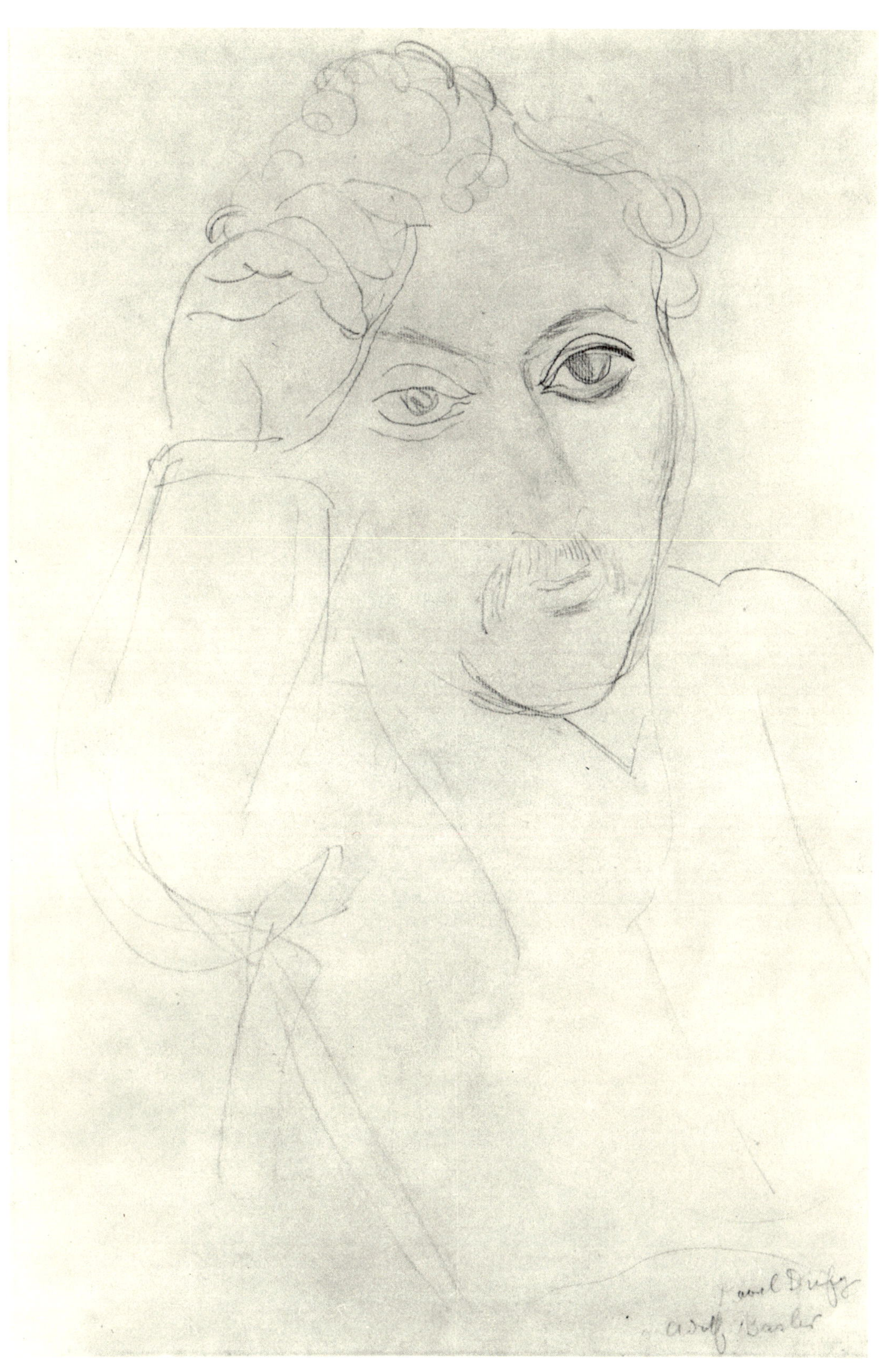

45 Raoul Dufy. *Adolphe Basler*

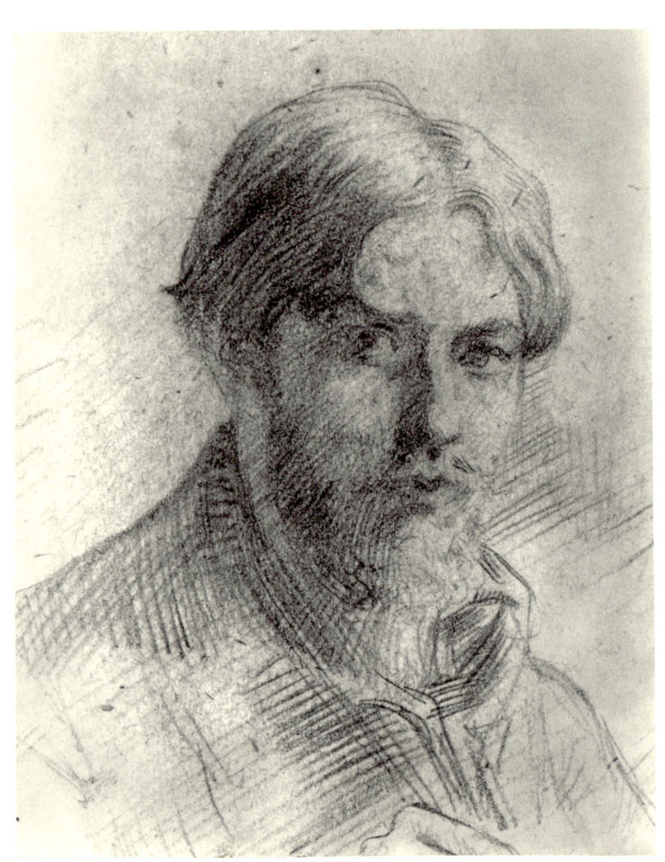

46 Sir Augustus John. *Self-Portrait*

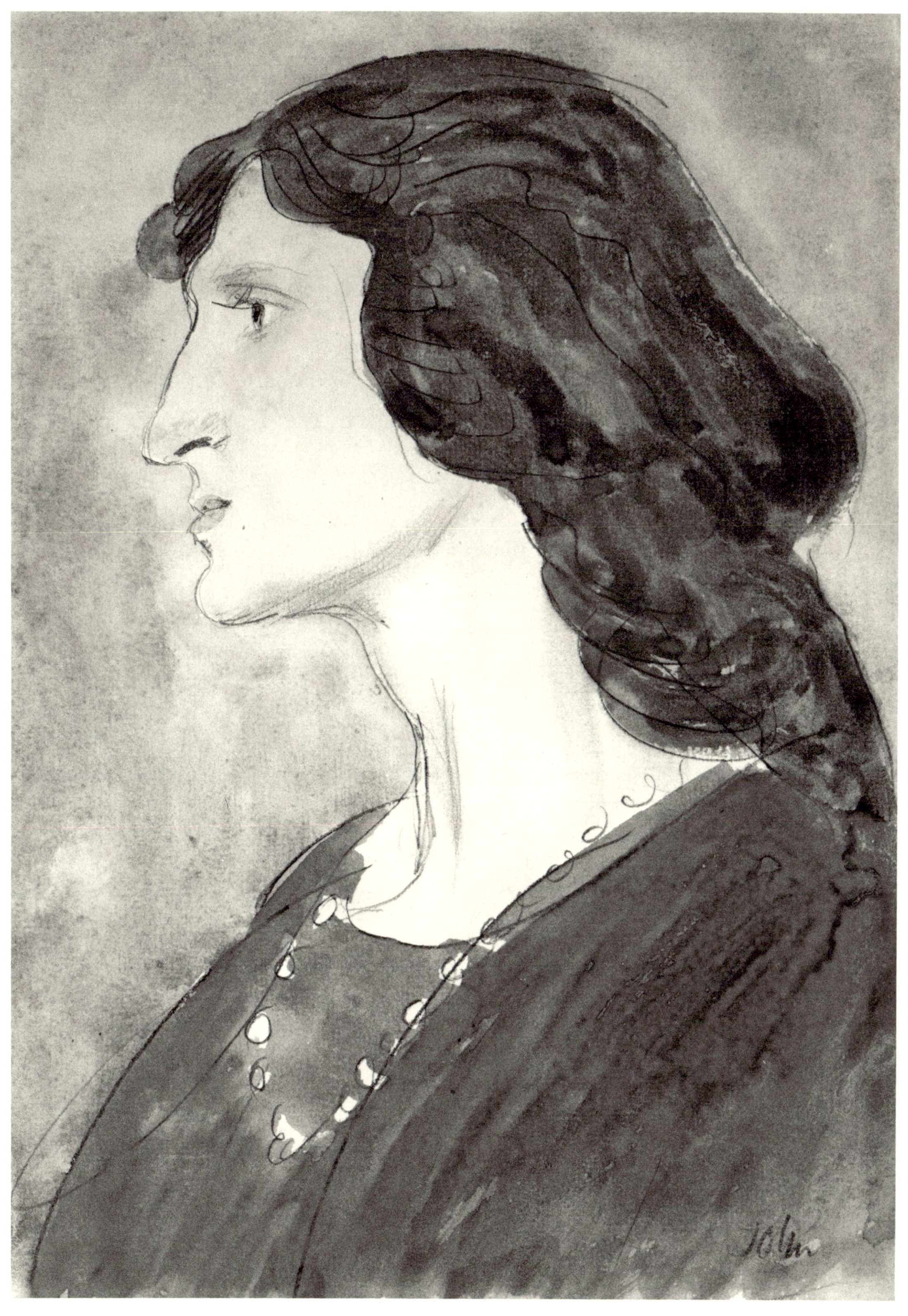

47 Sir Augustus John. *Lady Ottoline Morrell*

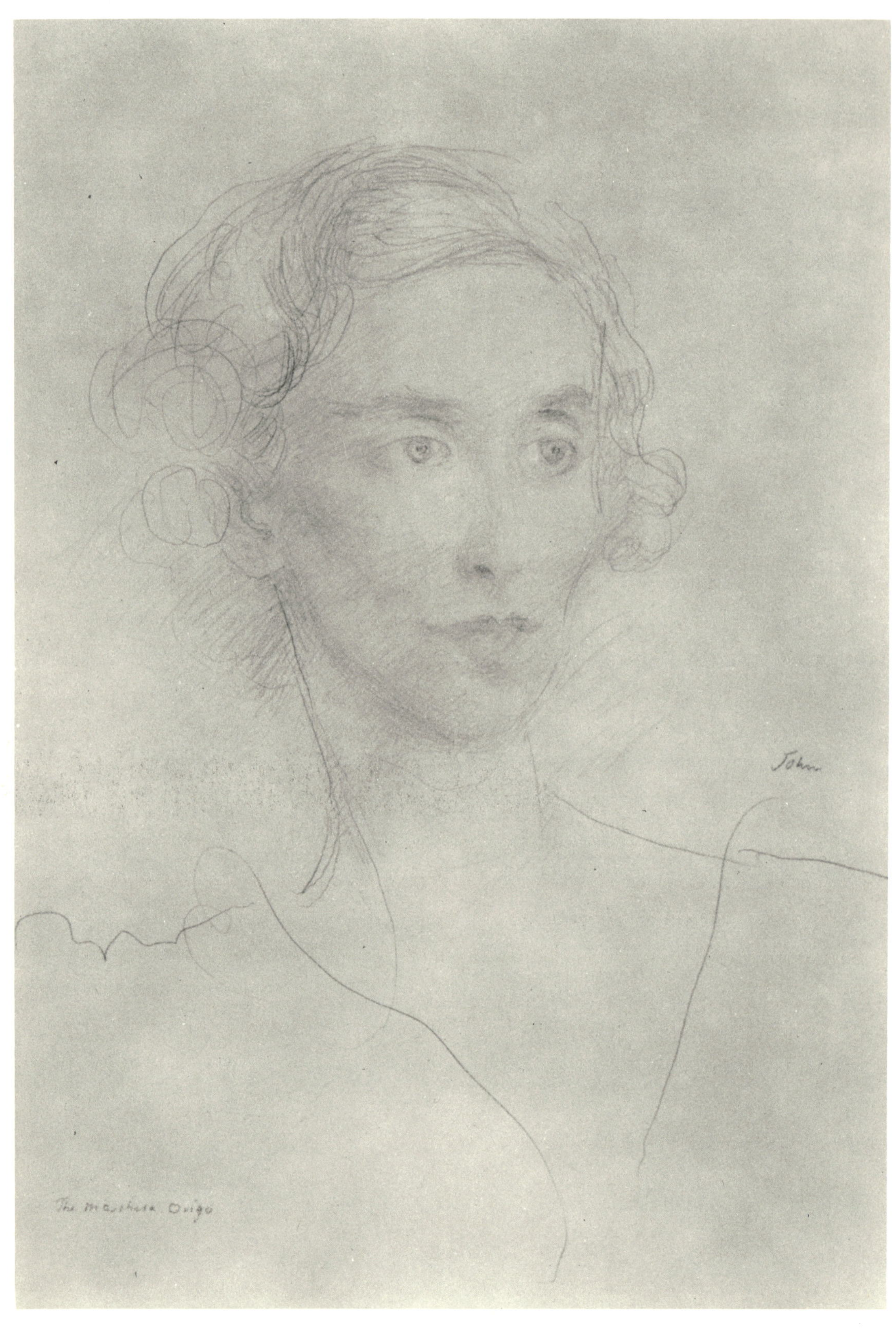

48 Sir Augustus John. *The Marchesa Origo*

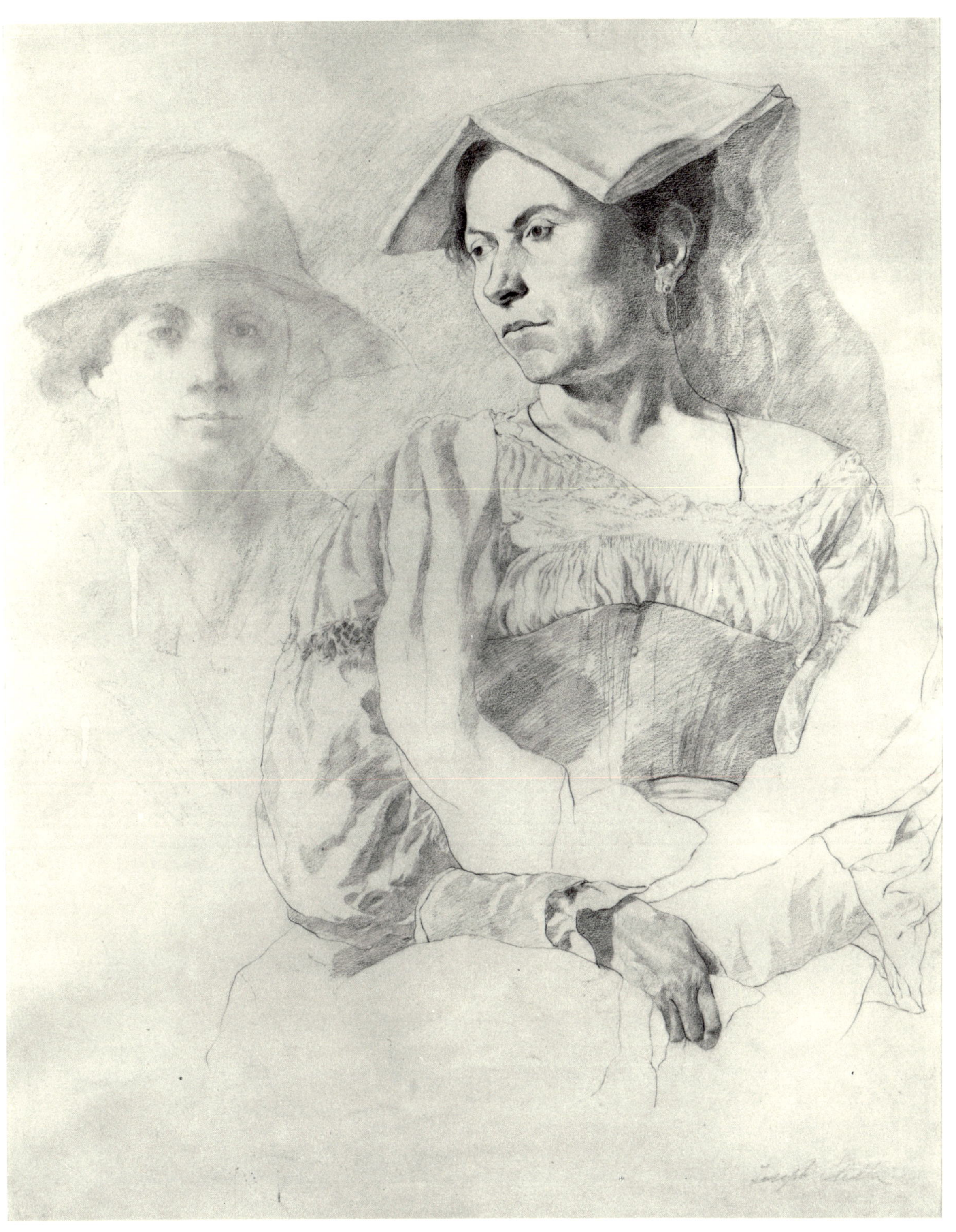

49 Joseph Stella. *Ellis Island Study: Young Couple*

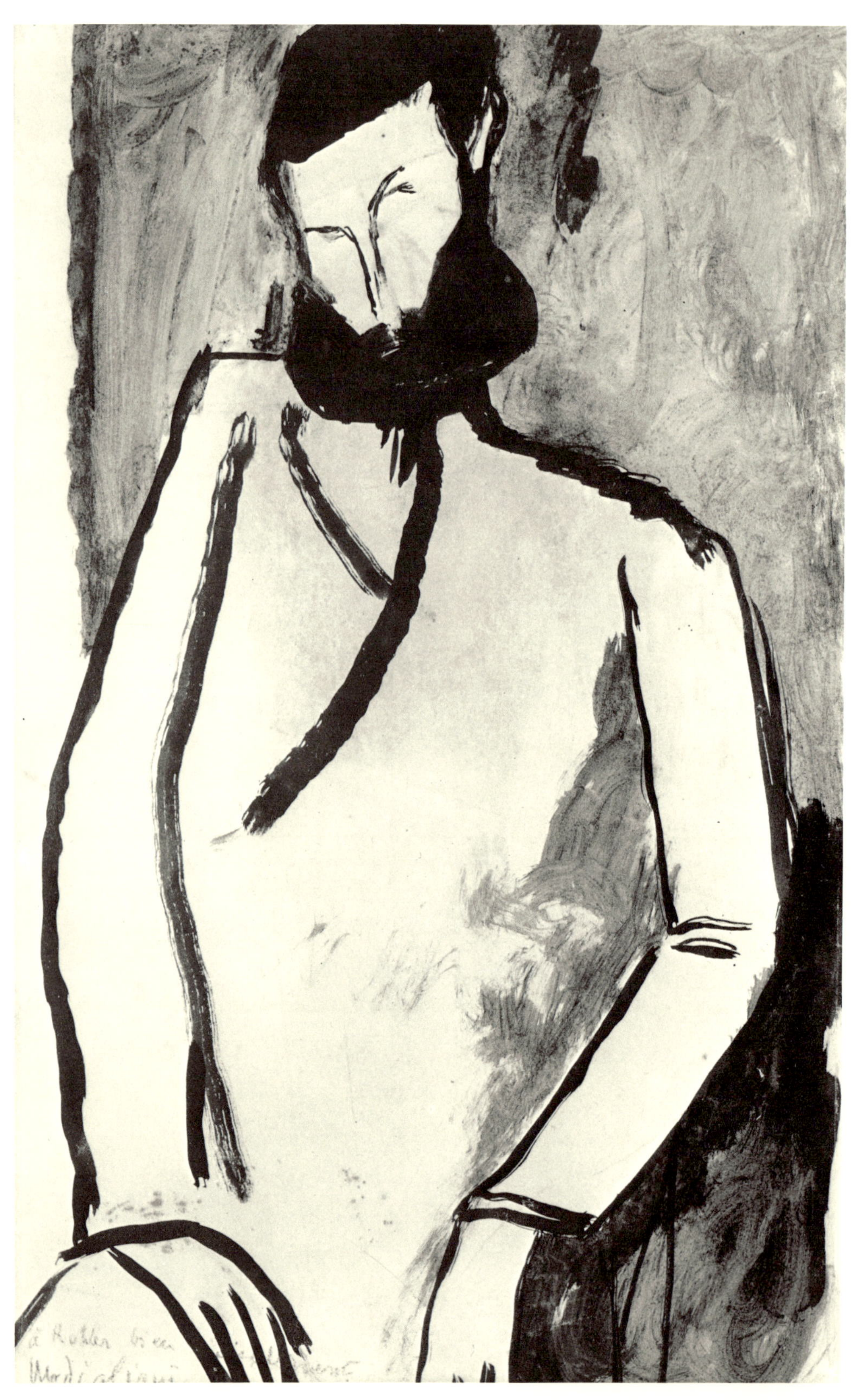

50 Amedeo Modigliani. *M. Kohler*

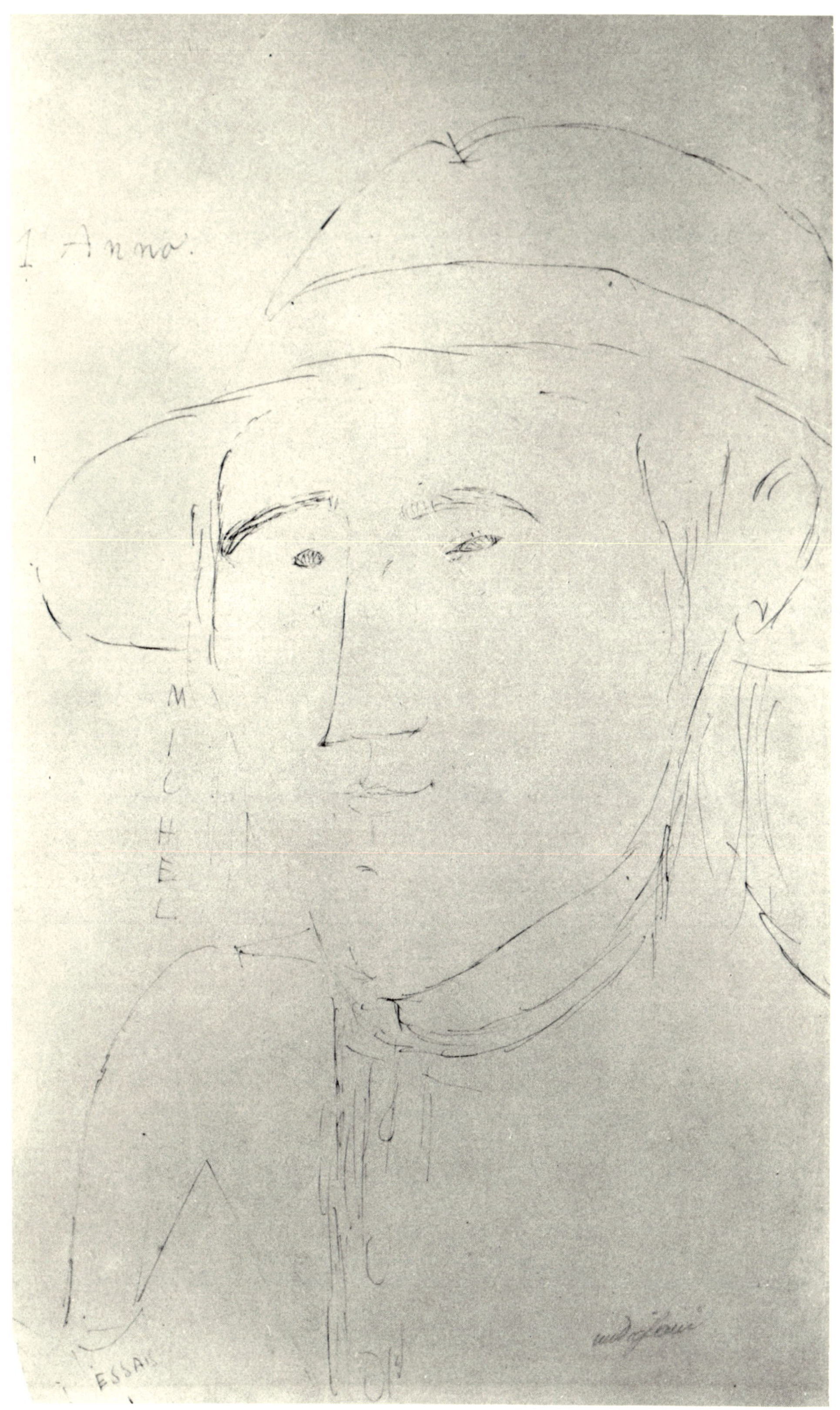

51 Amedeo Modigliani. *Michel*

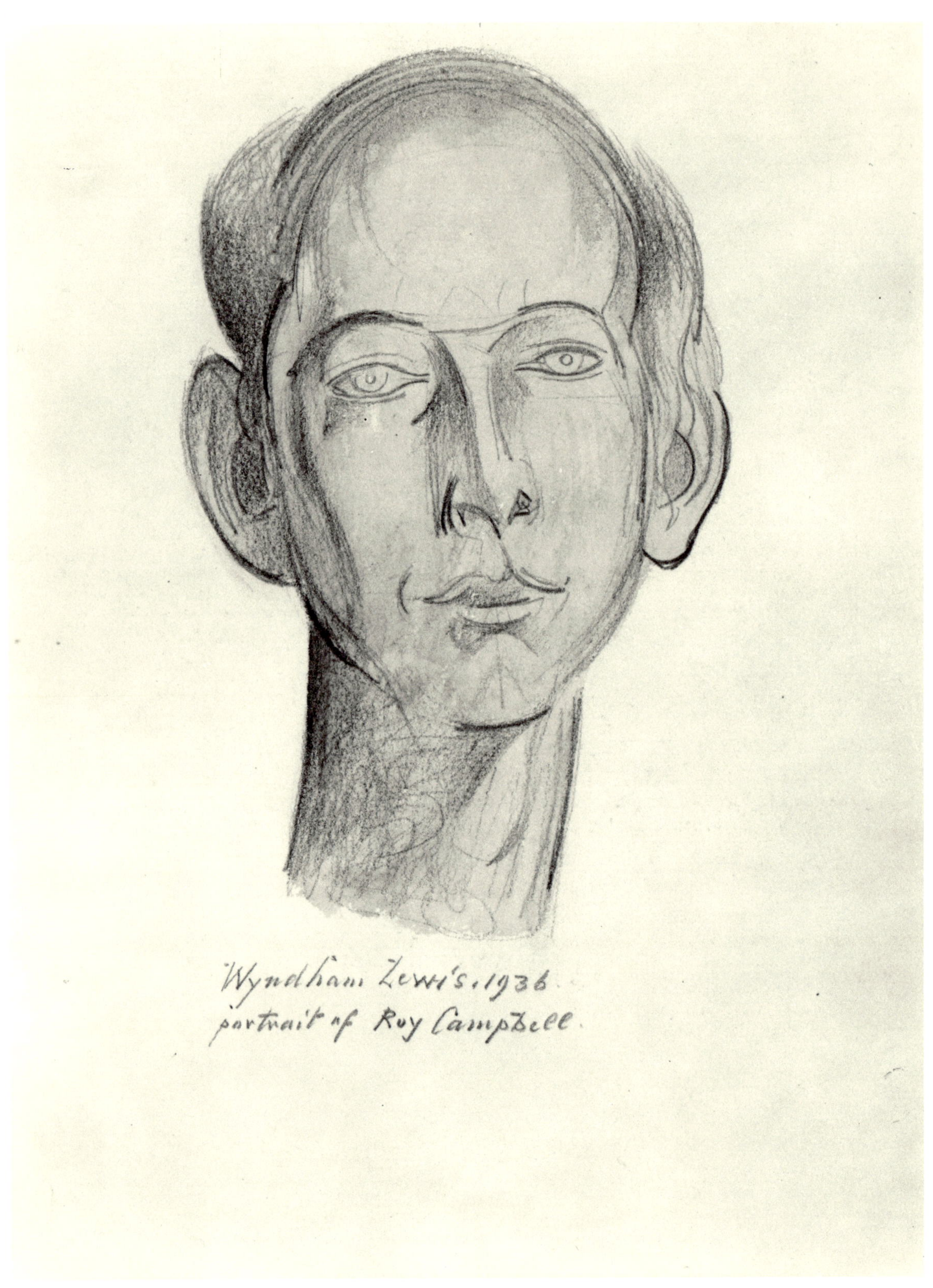

52 Wyndham Lewis. *Roy Campbell*

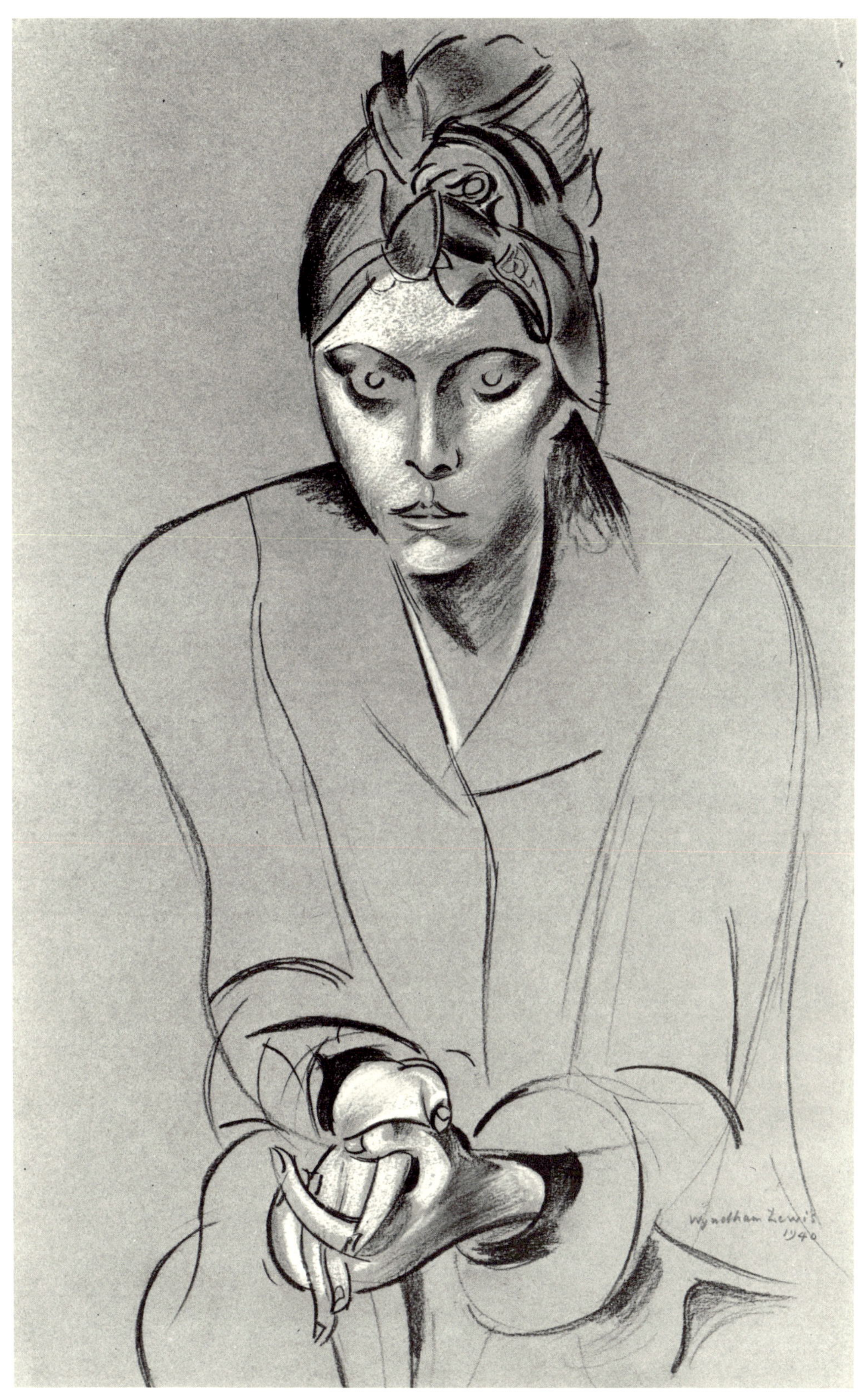

53 Wyndham Lewis. *Mrs. Lewis*

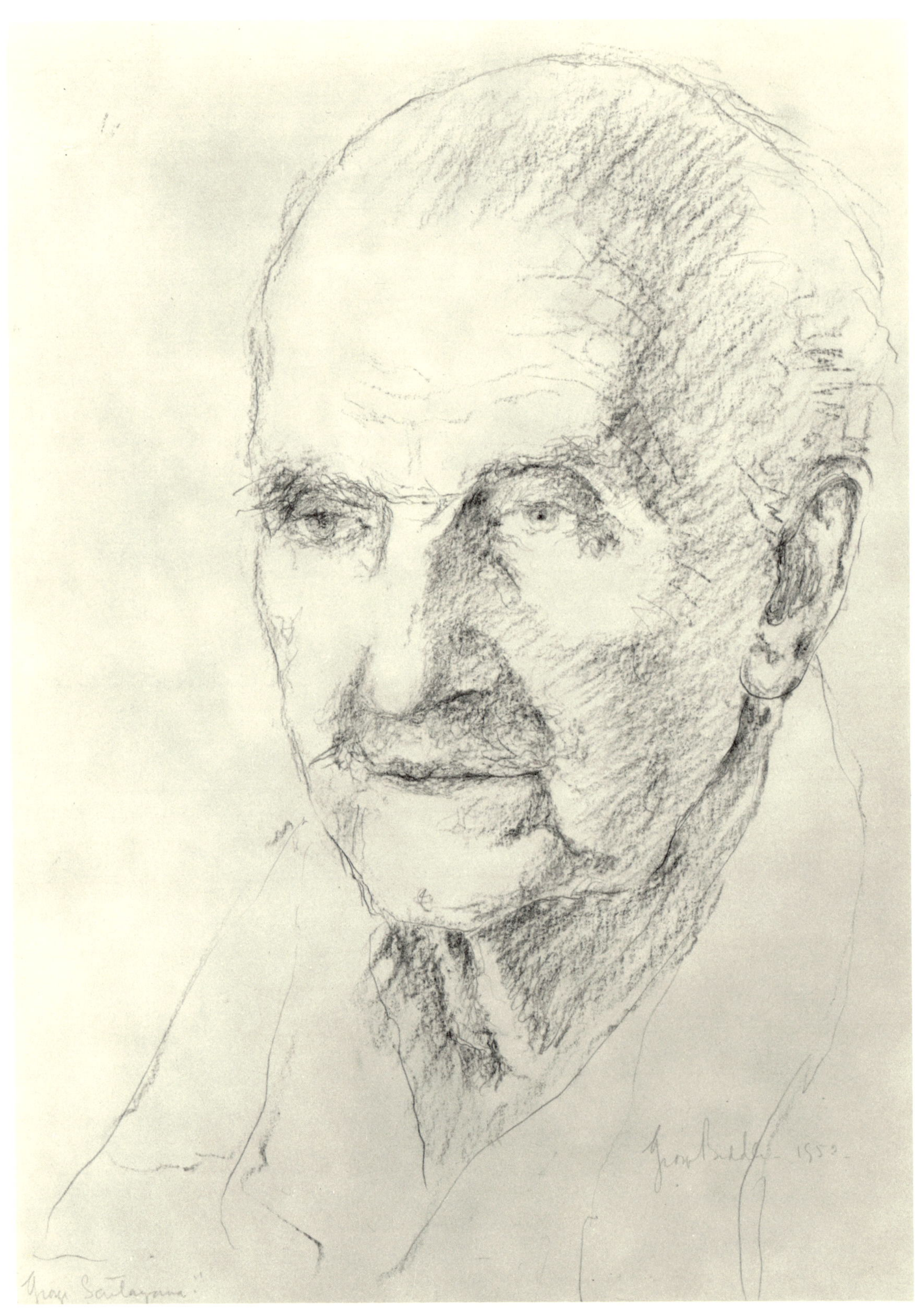

54 George Biddle. *George Santayana*

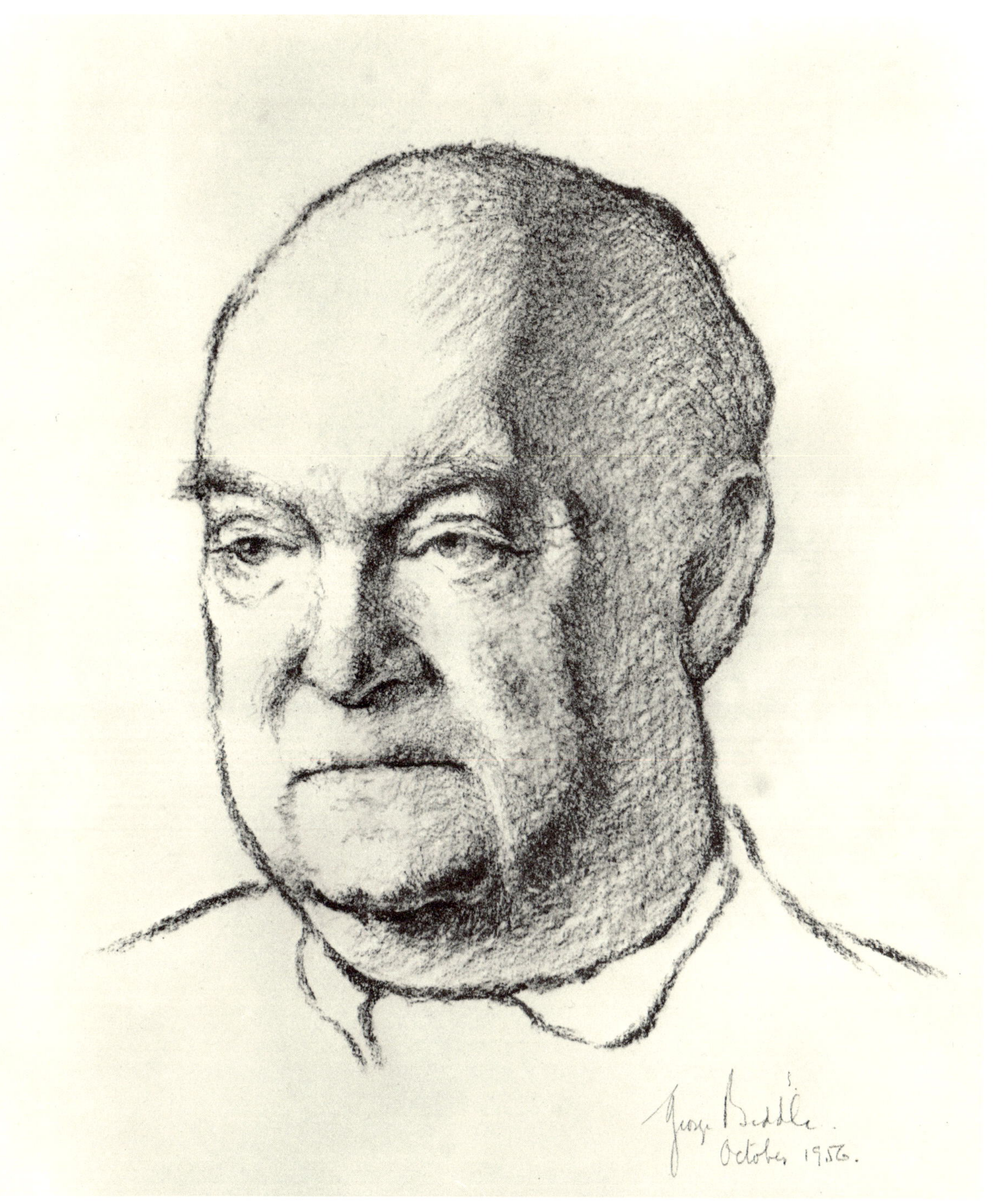

55 George Biddle. *Edmund Wilson*

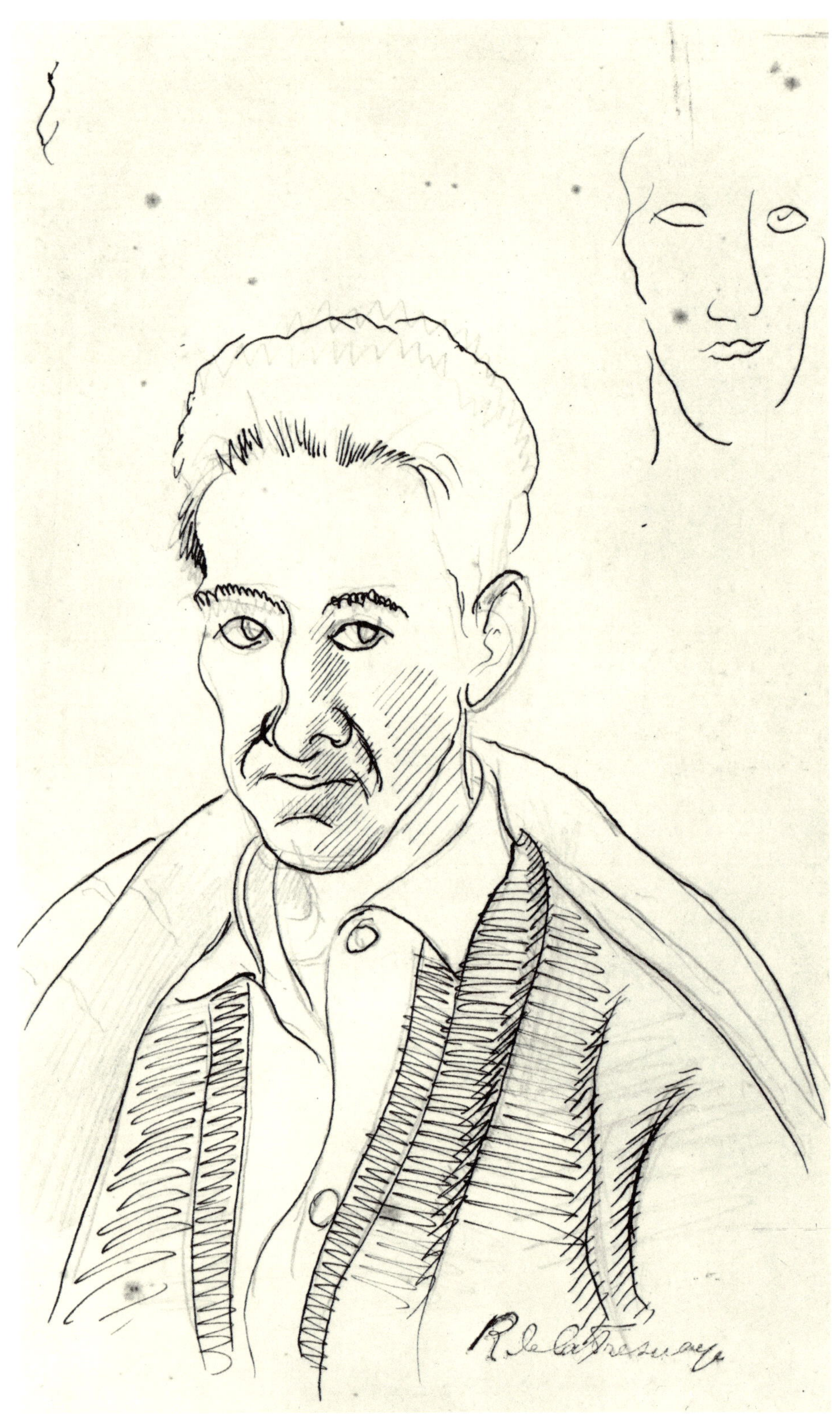

56 Roger de La Fresnaye. *Self-Portrait*

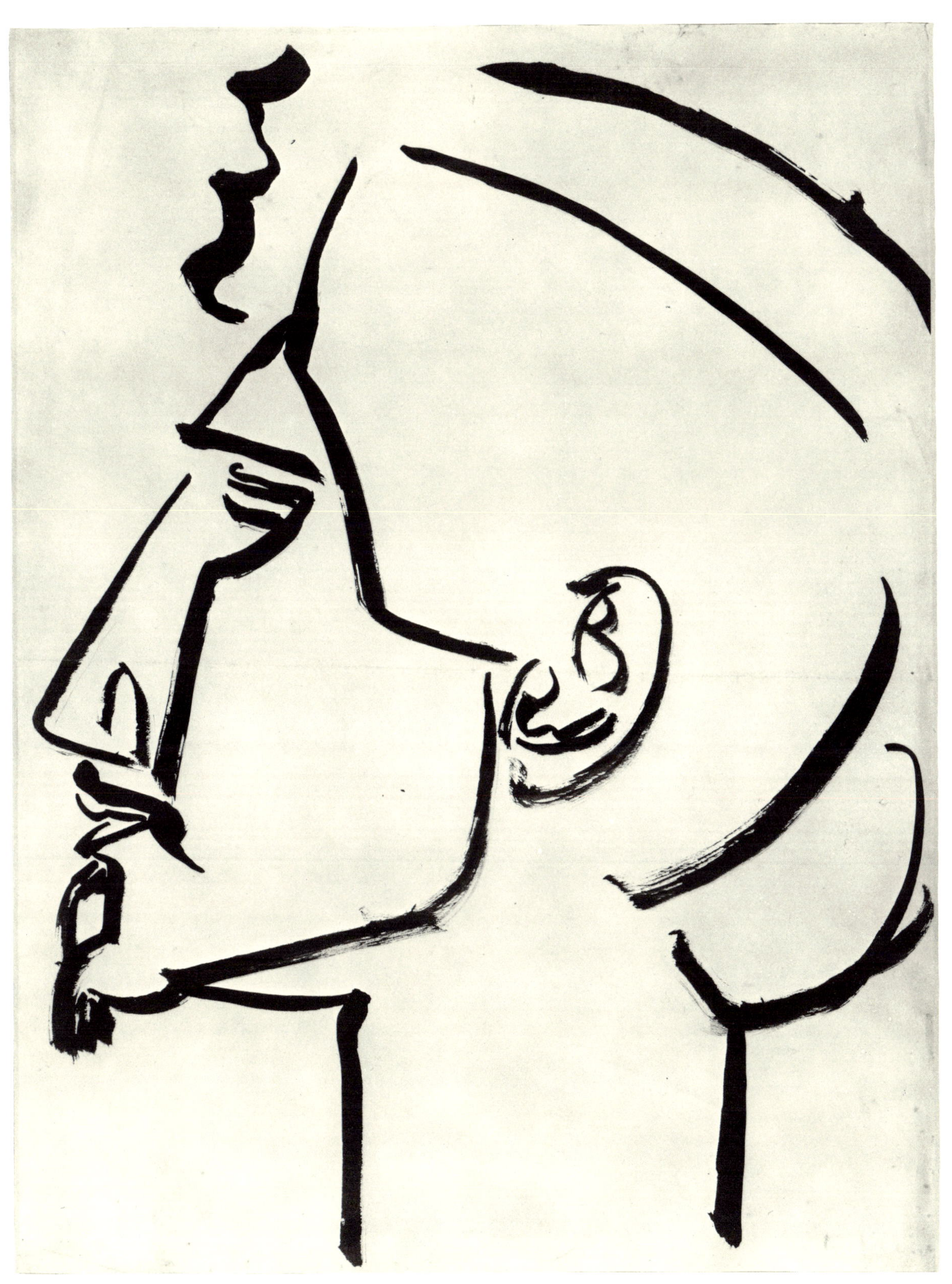

57 Henri Gaudier-Brzeska. *Ezra Pound*

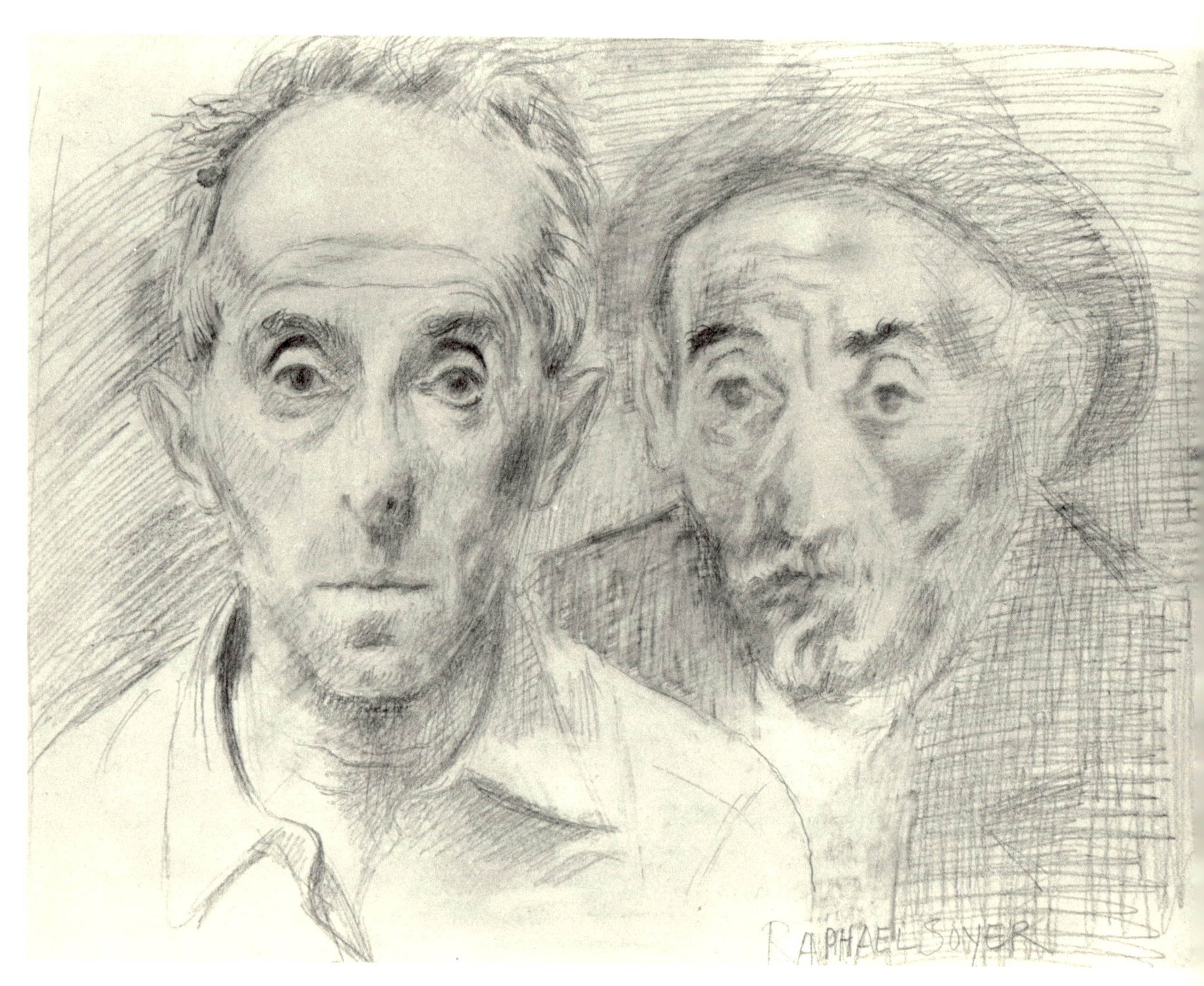

58 Raphael Soyer. *Self-Portrait with the Artist's Father*

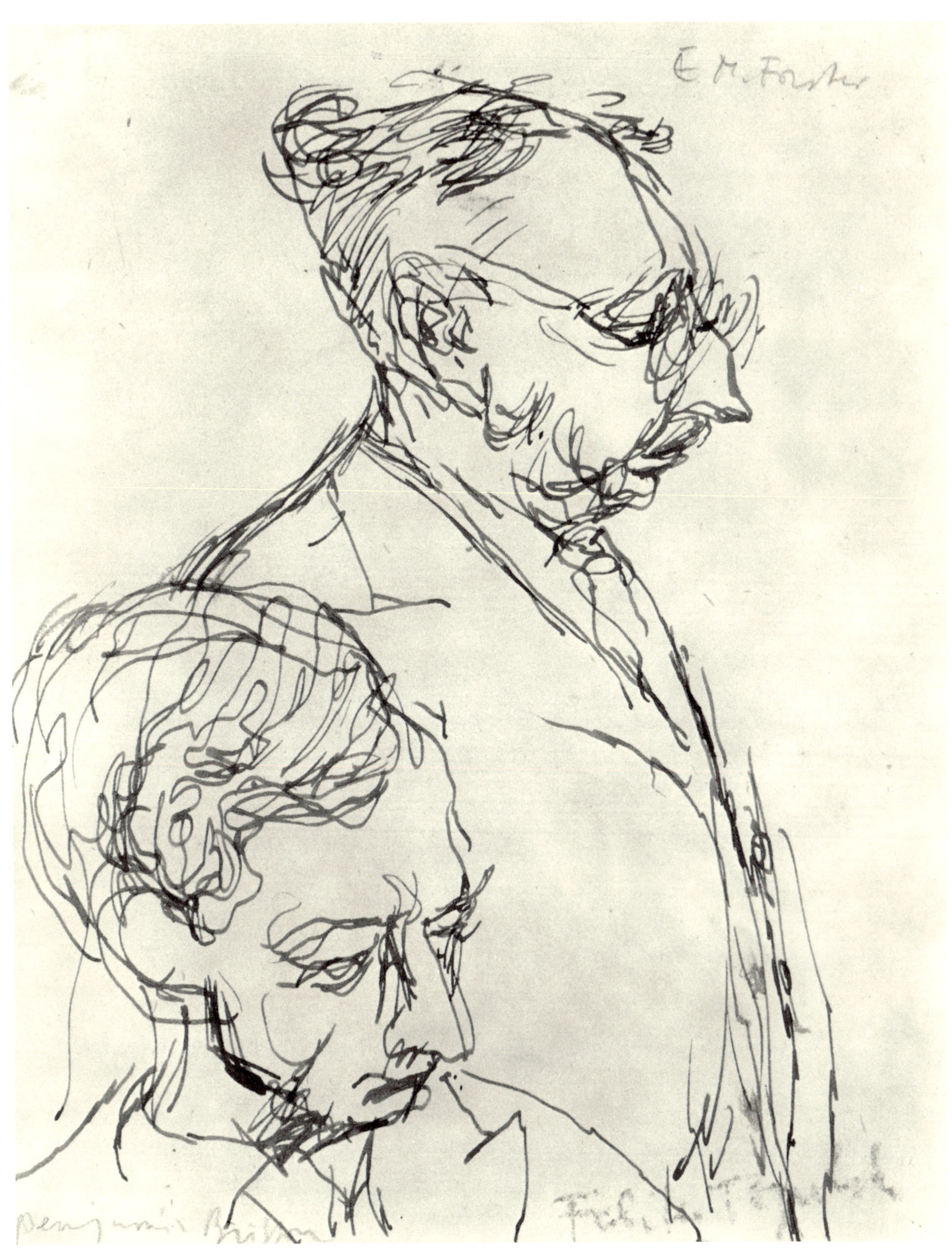

59 Feliks Topolski. *E. M. Forster and Benjamin Britten*

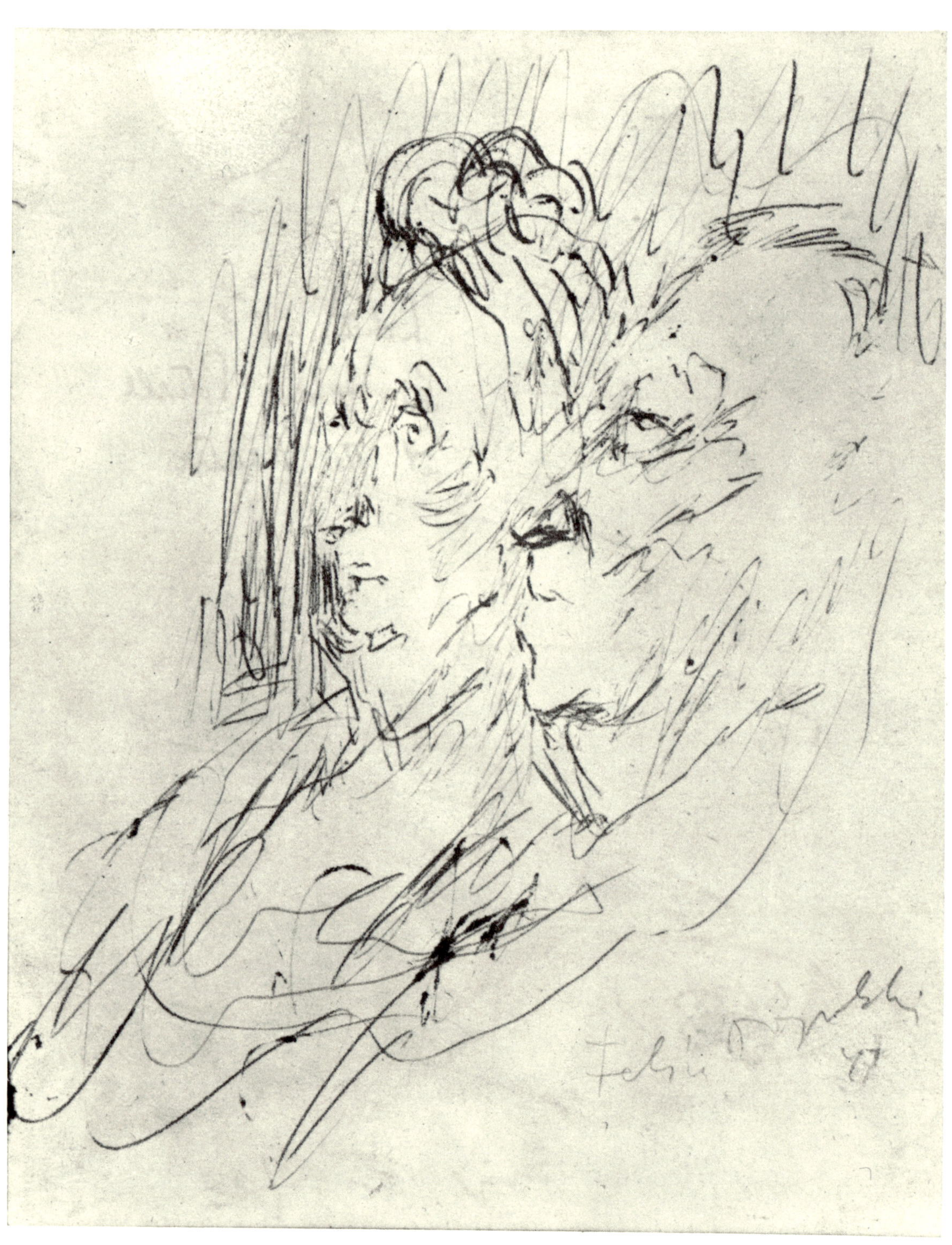

60 Feliks Topolski. *Dame Edith and Sir Osbert Sitwell*

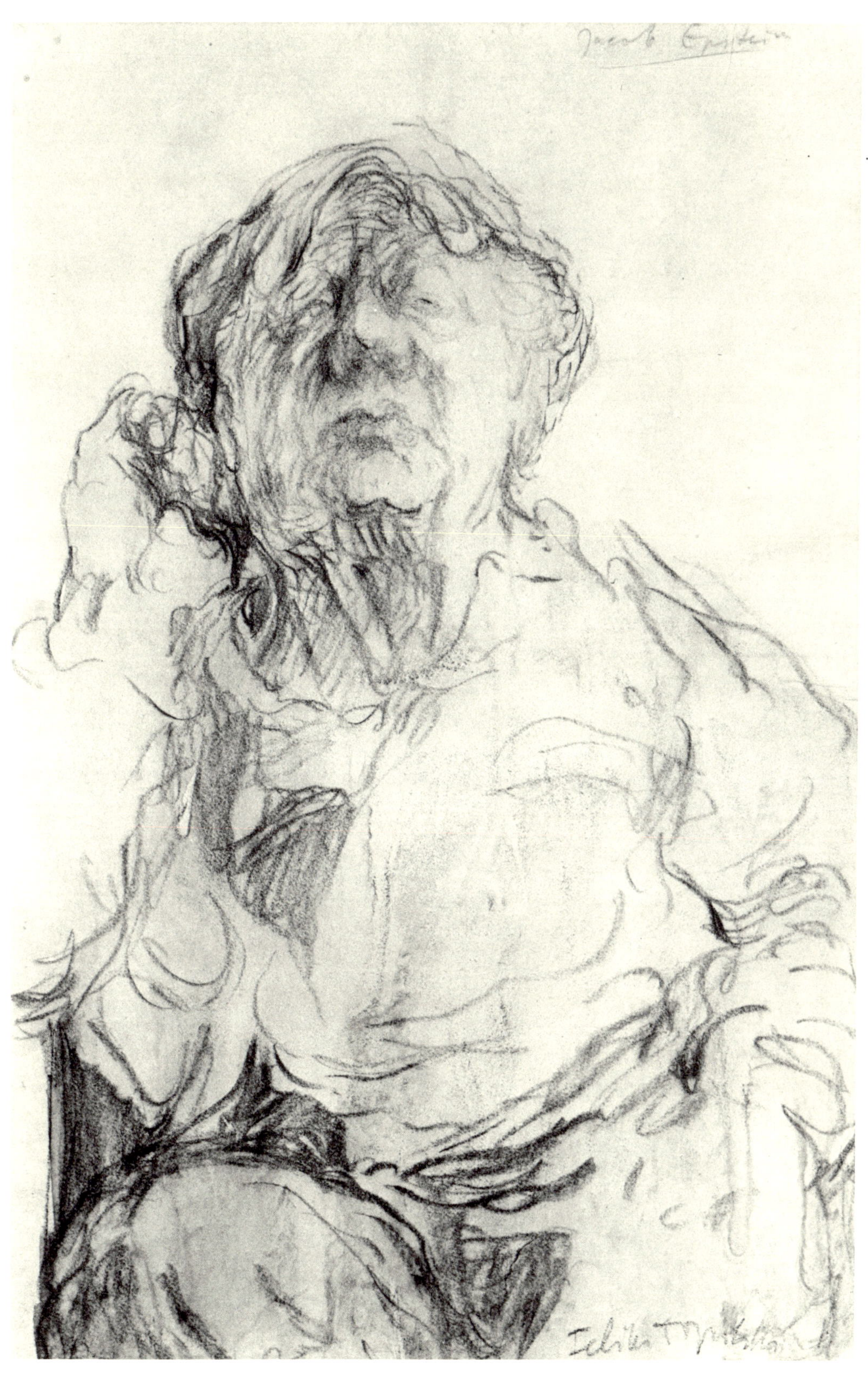

61 Feliks Topolski. *Sir Jacob Epstein*

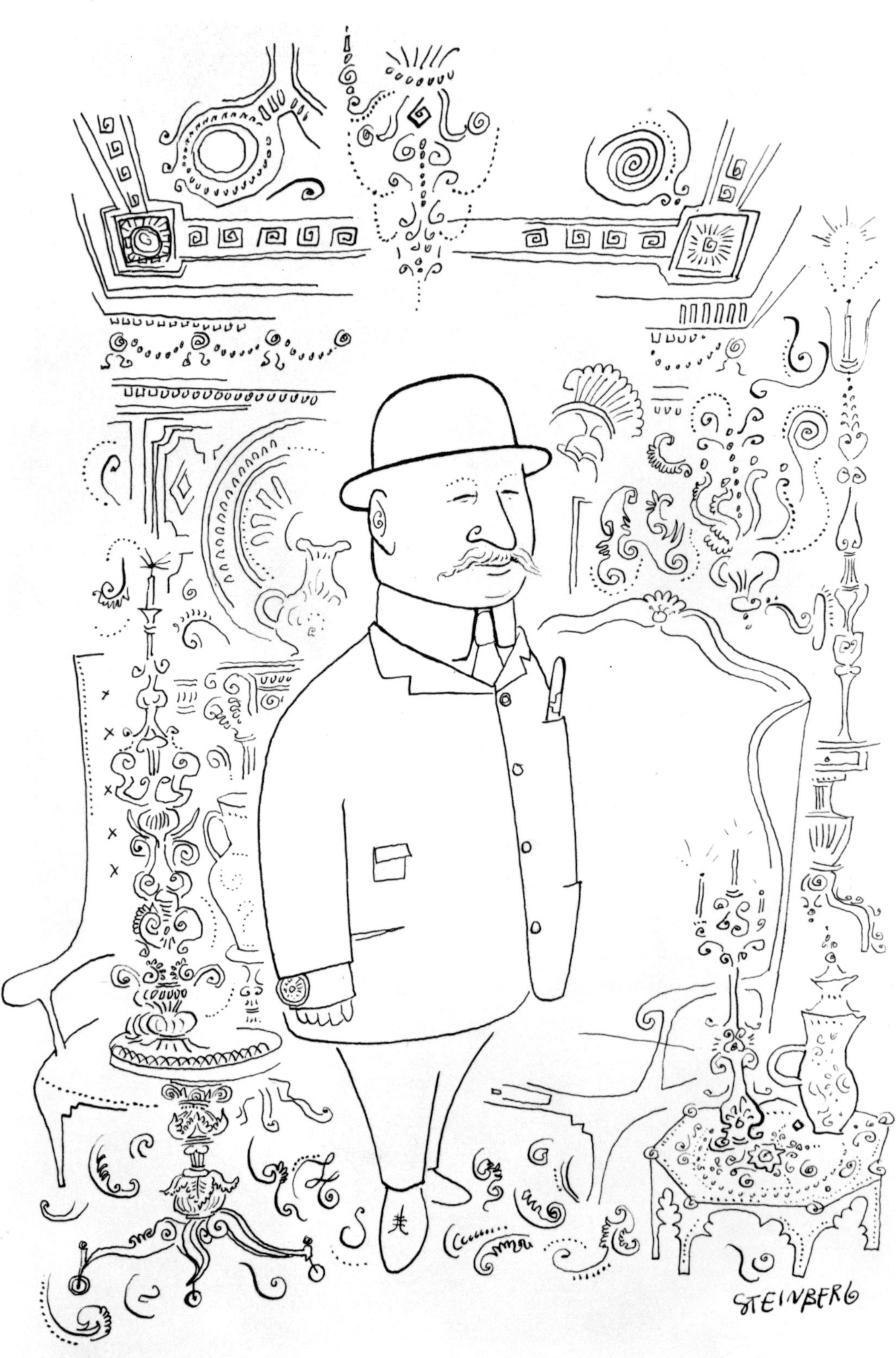

62 Saul Steinberg. *Benjamin Sonnenberg*

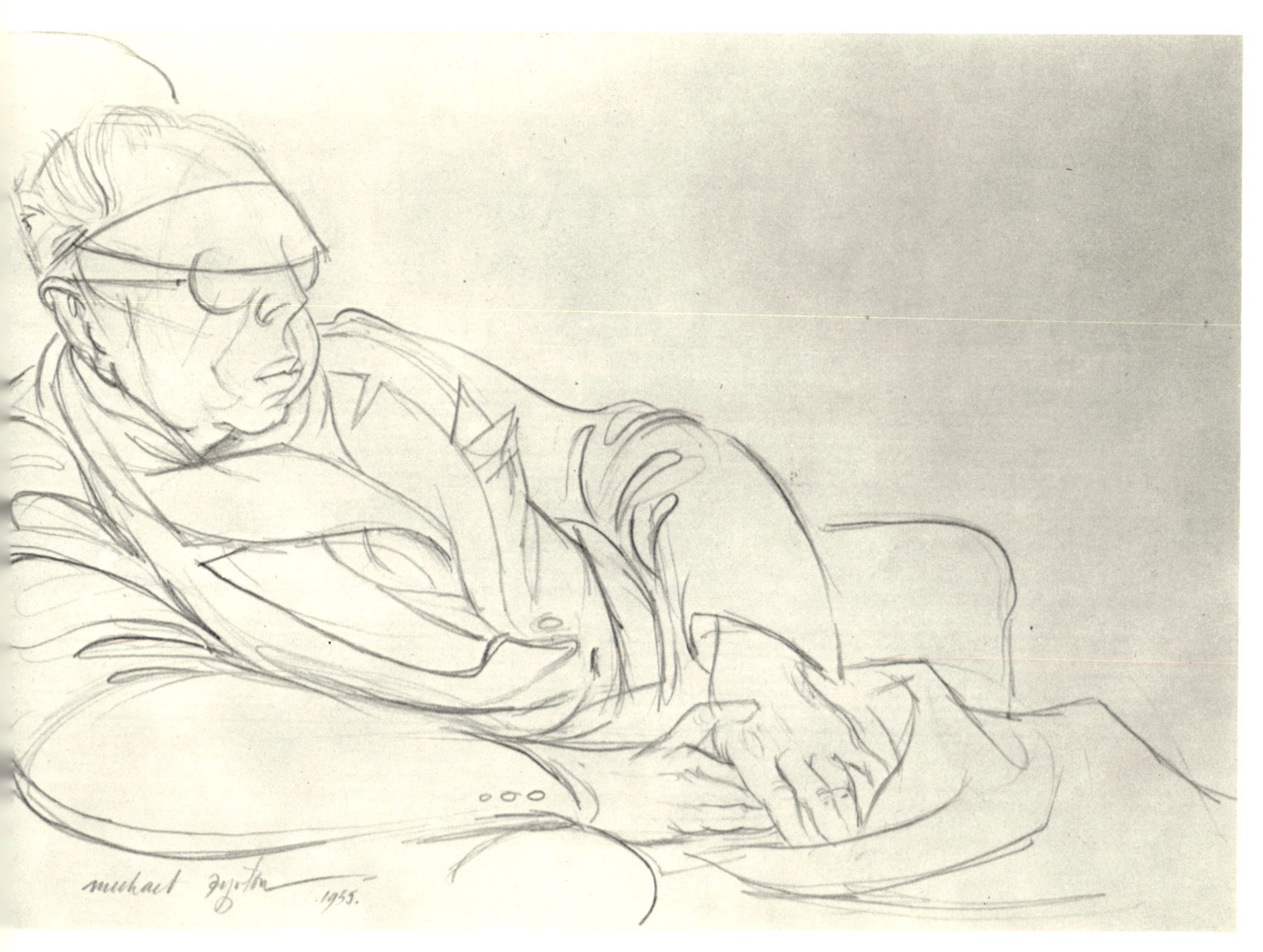

63 Michael Ayrton. *Wyndham Lewis*

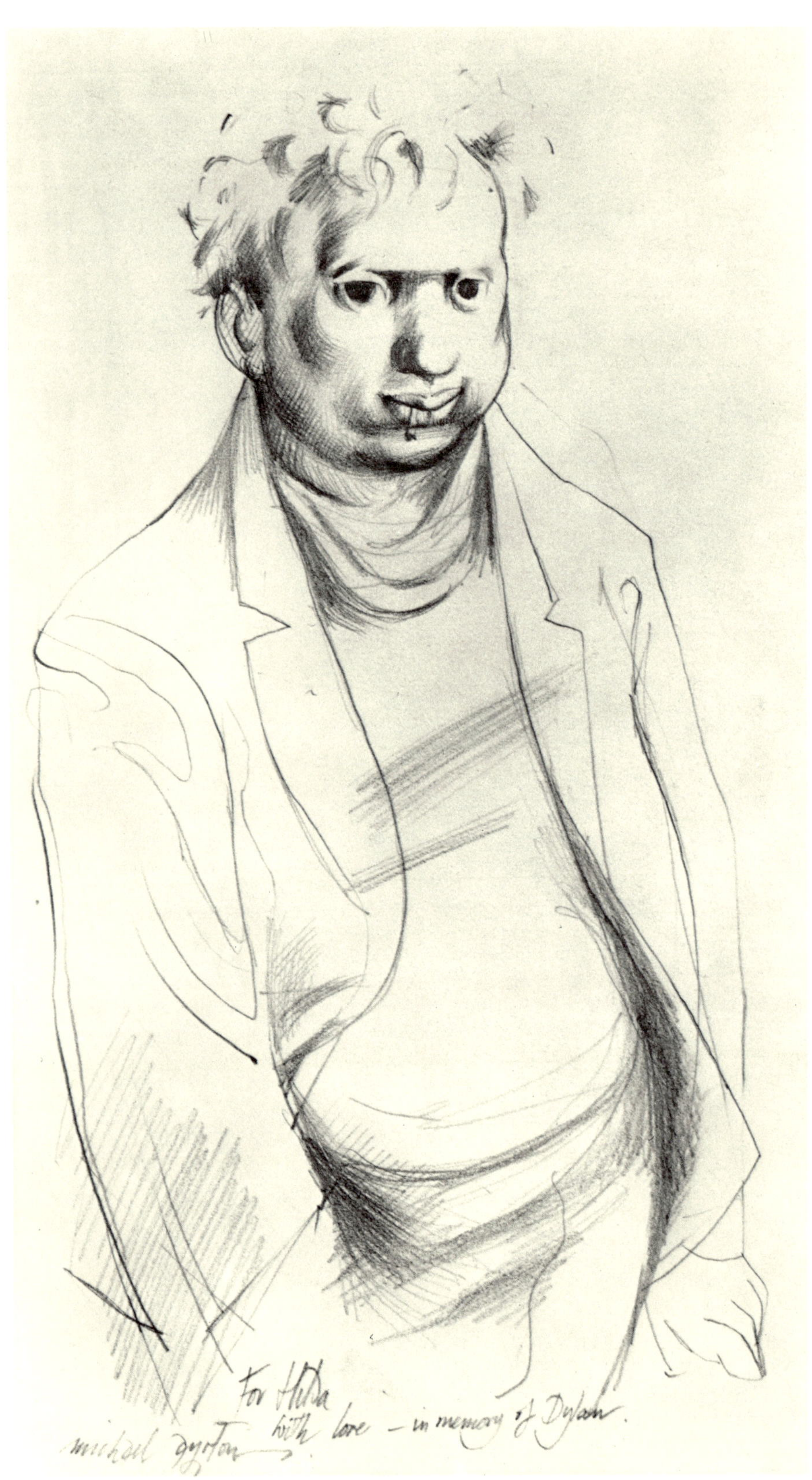

64 Michael Ayrton. *Dylan Thomas*

This catalogue of the exhibition, *Artists and Writers*, has been published in an edition of seventeen hundred and fifty copies designed and printed at The Spiral Press in New York City, with plates by The Meriden Gravure Company, Meriden, Connecticut.